QT WORLD

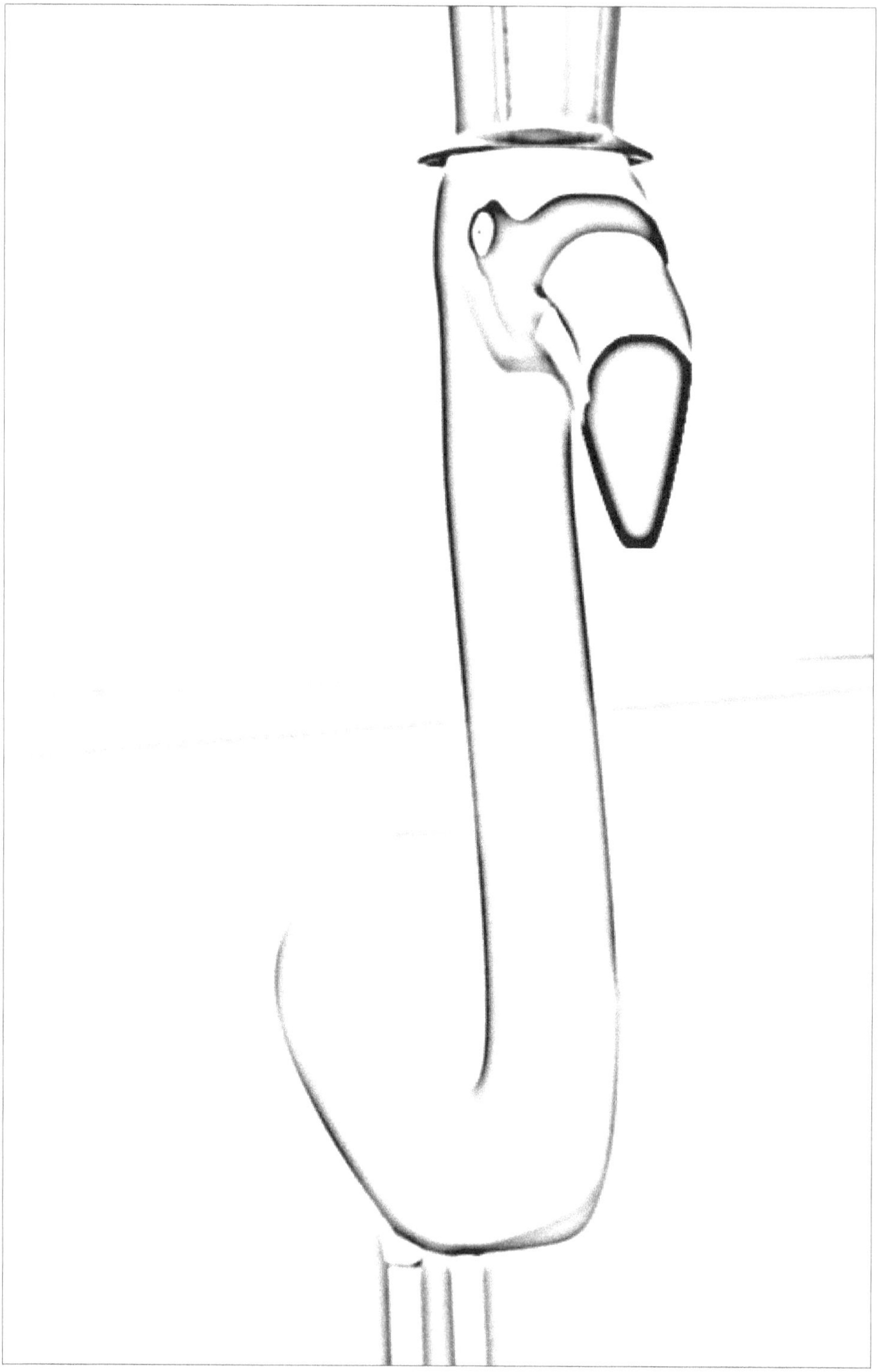

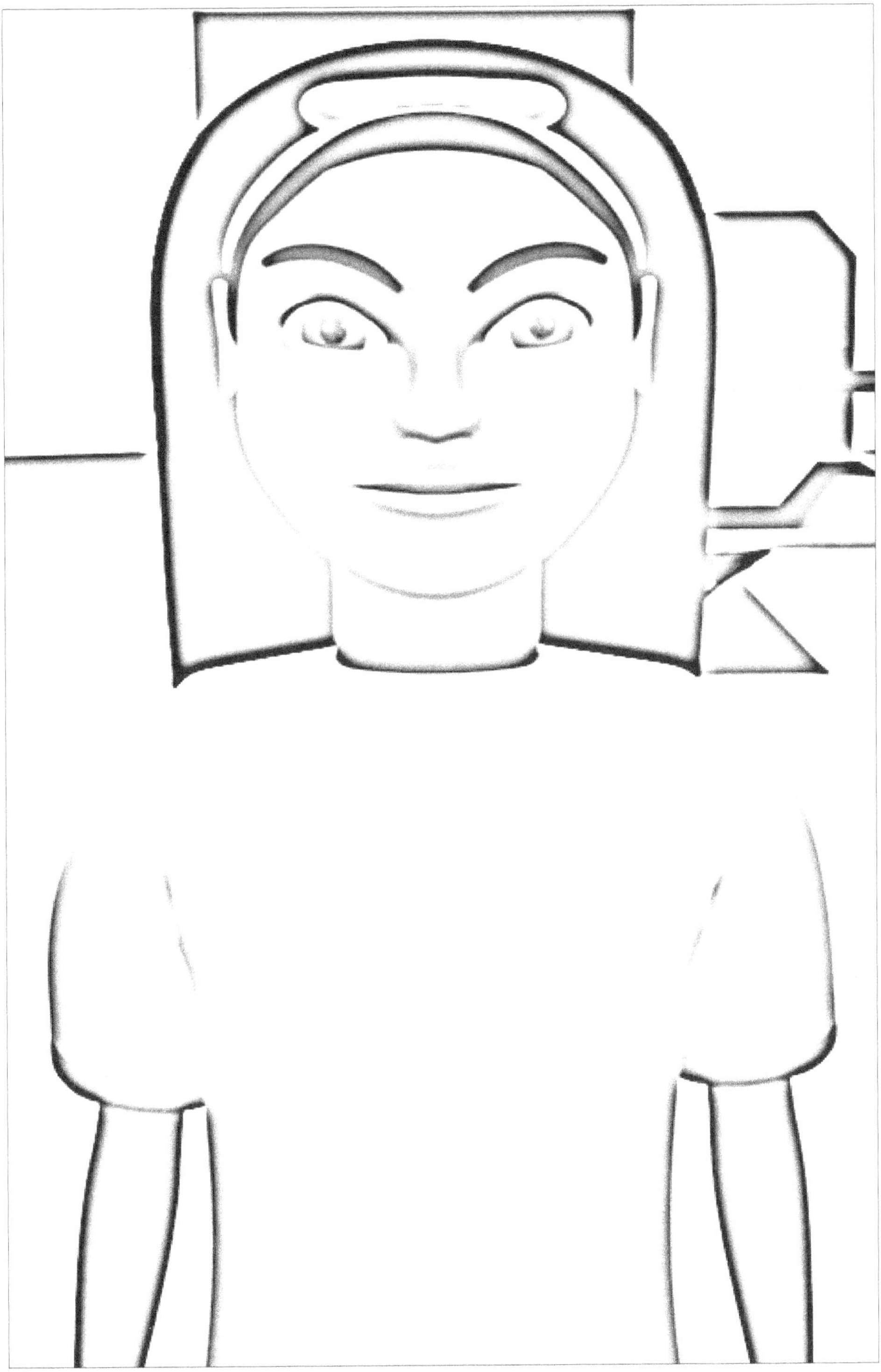

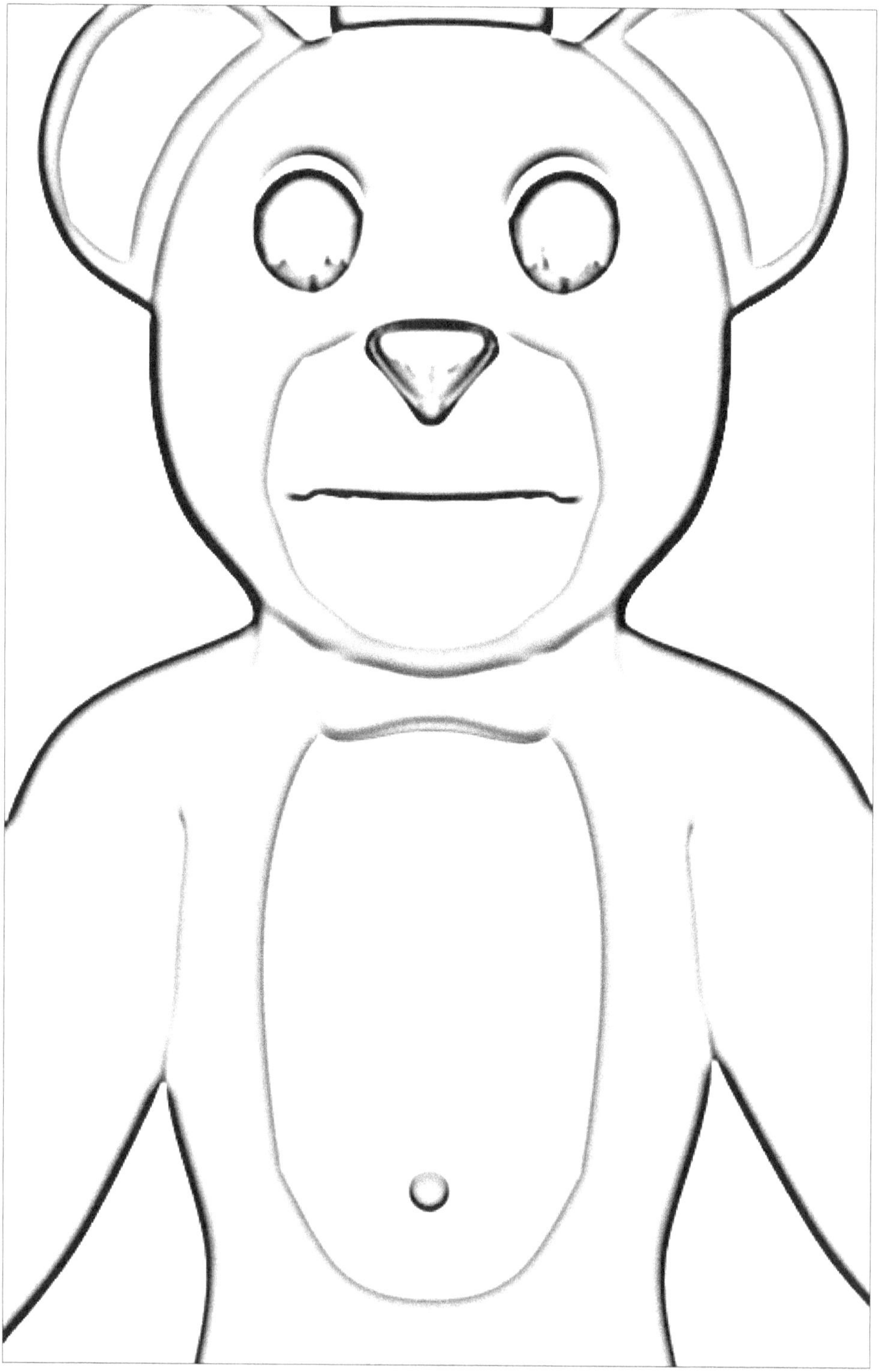

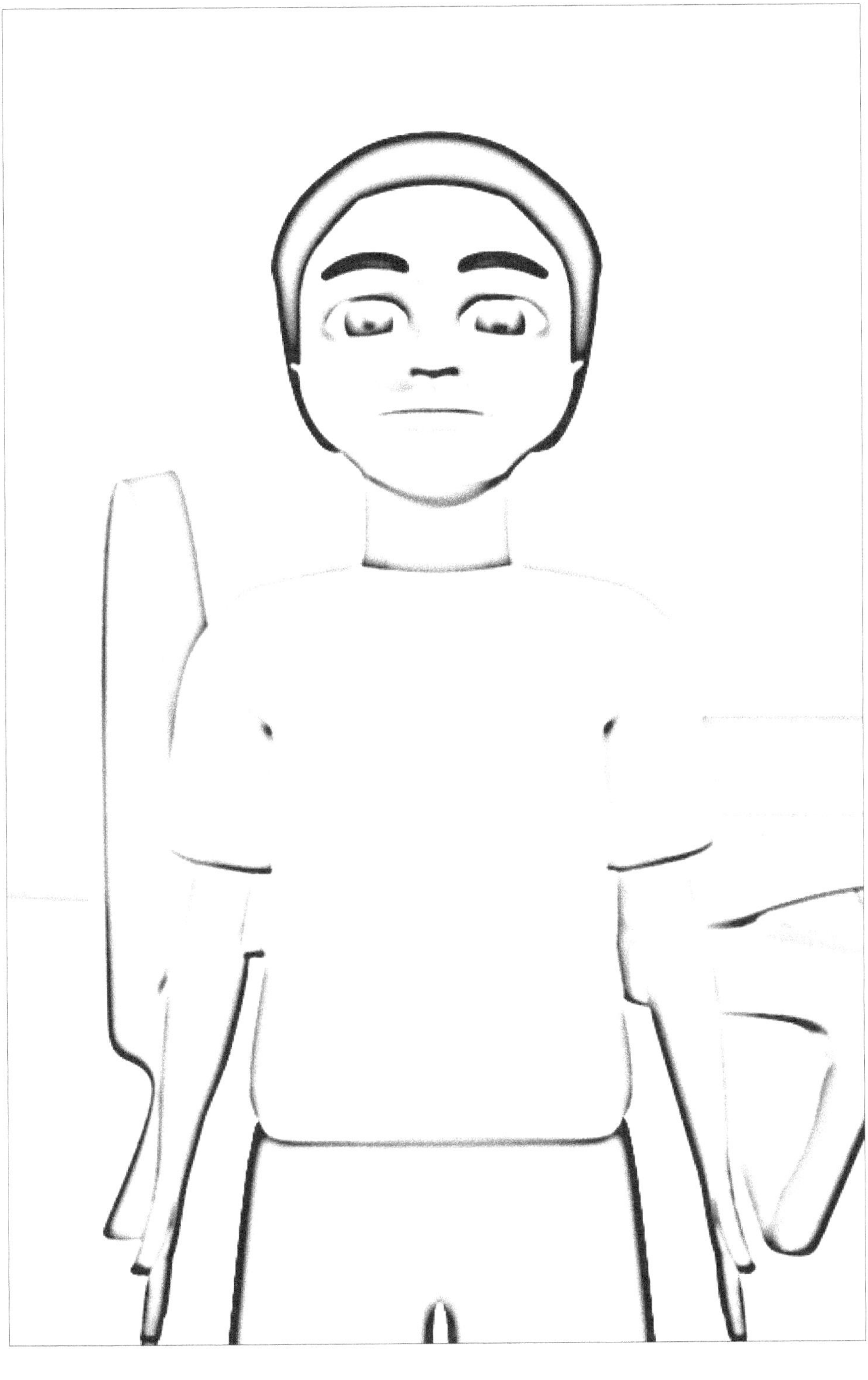

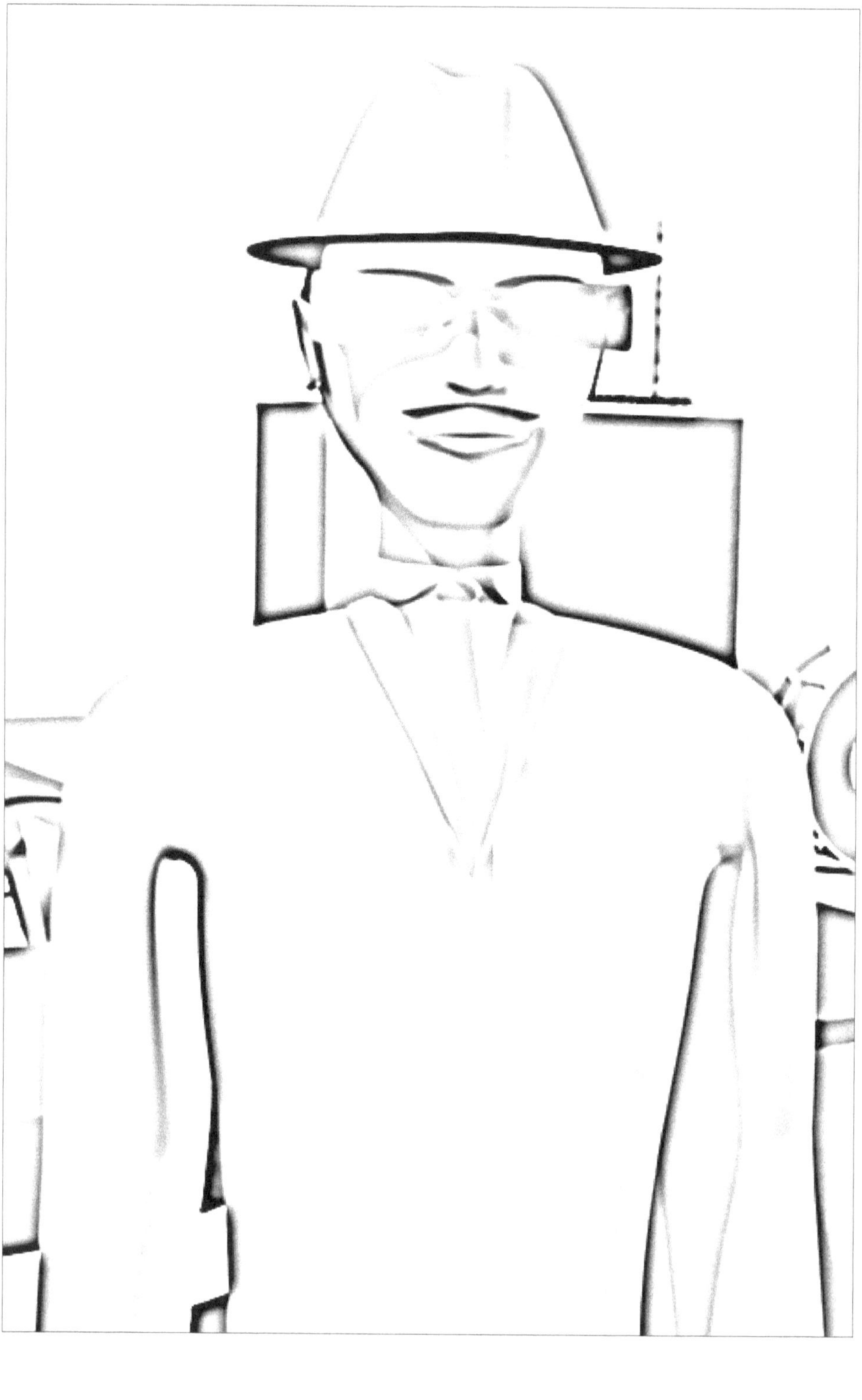

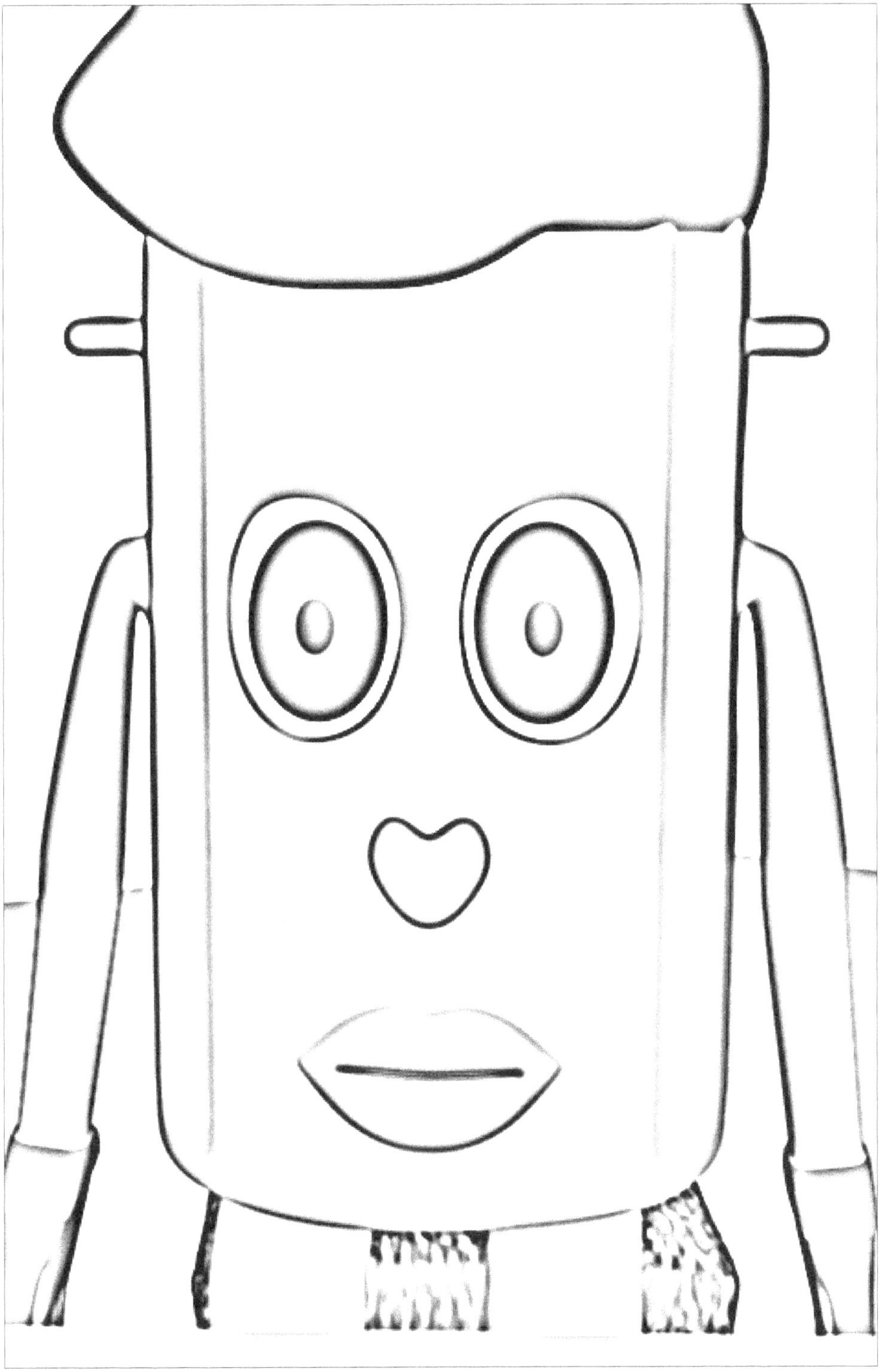

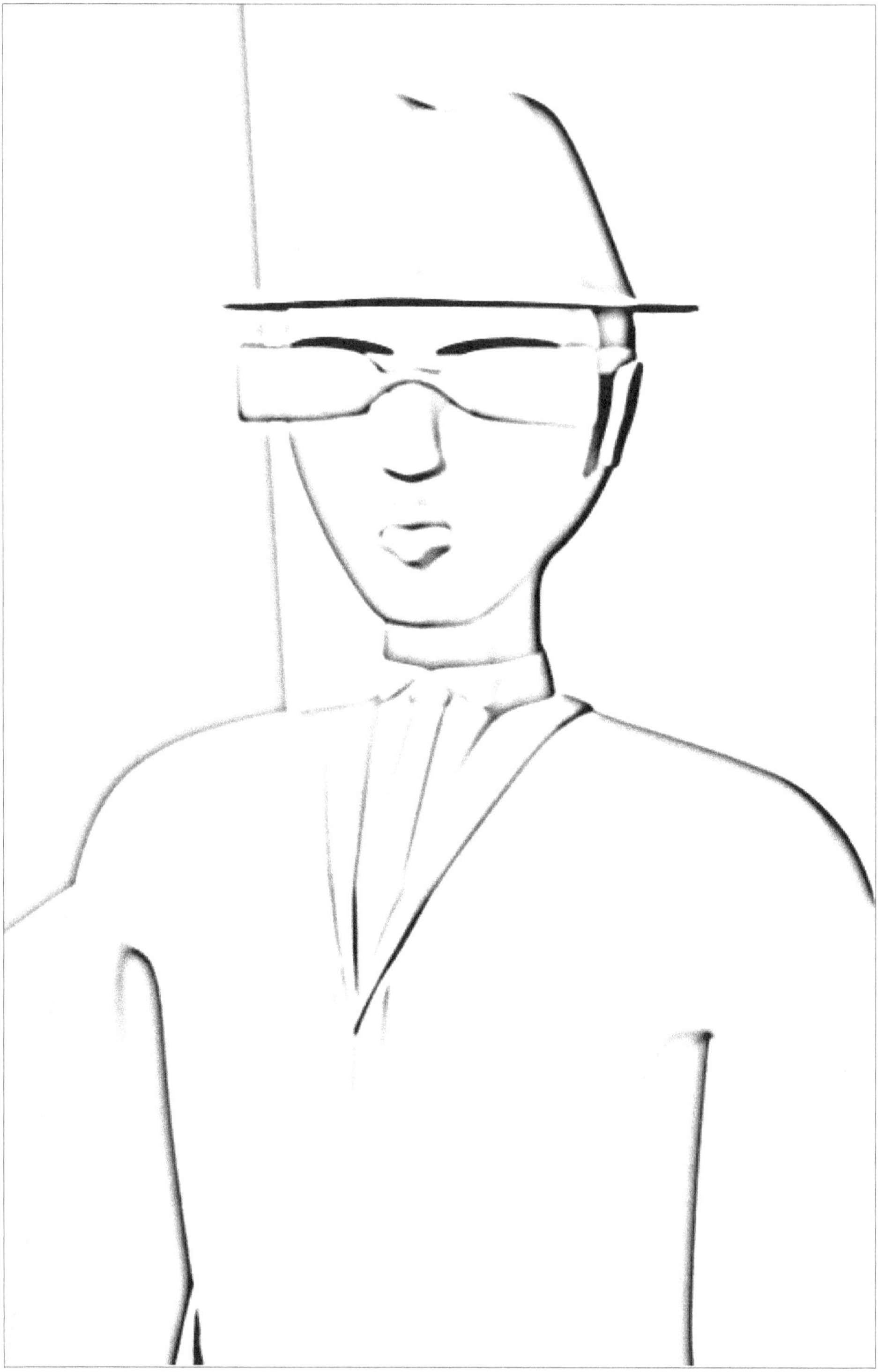

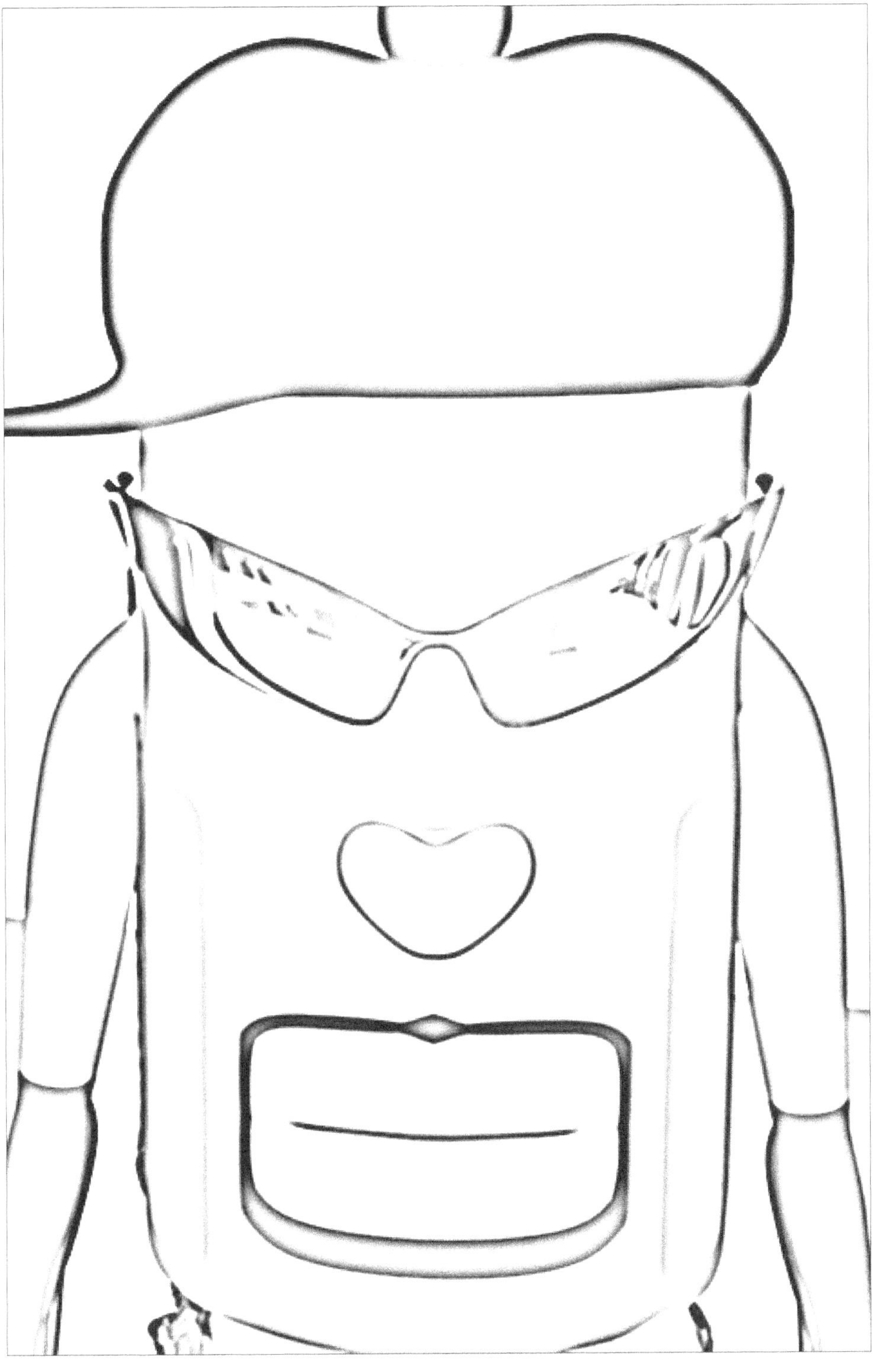

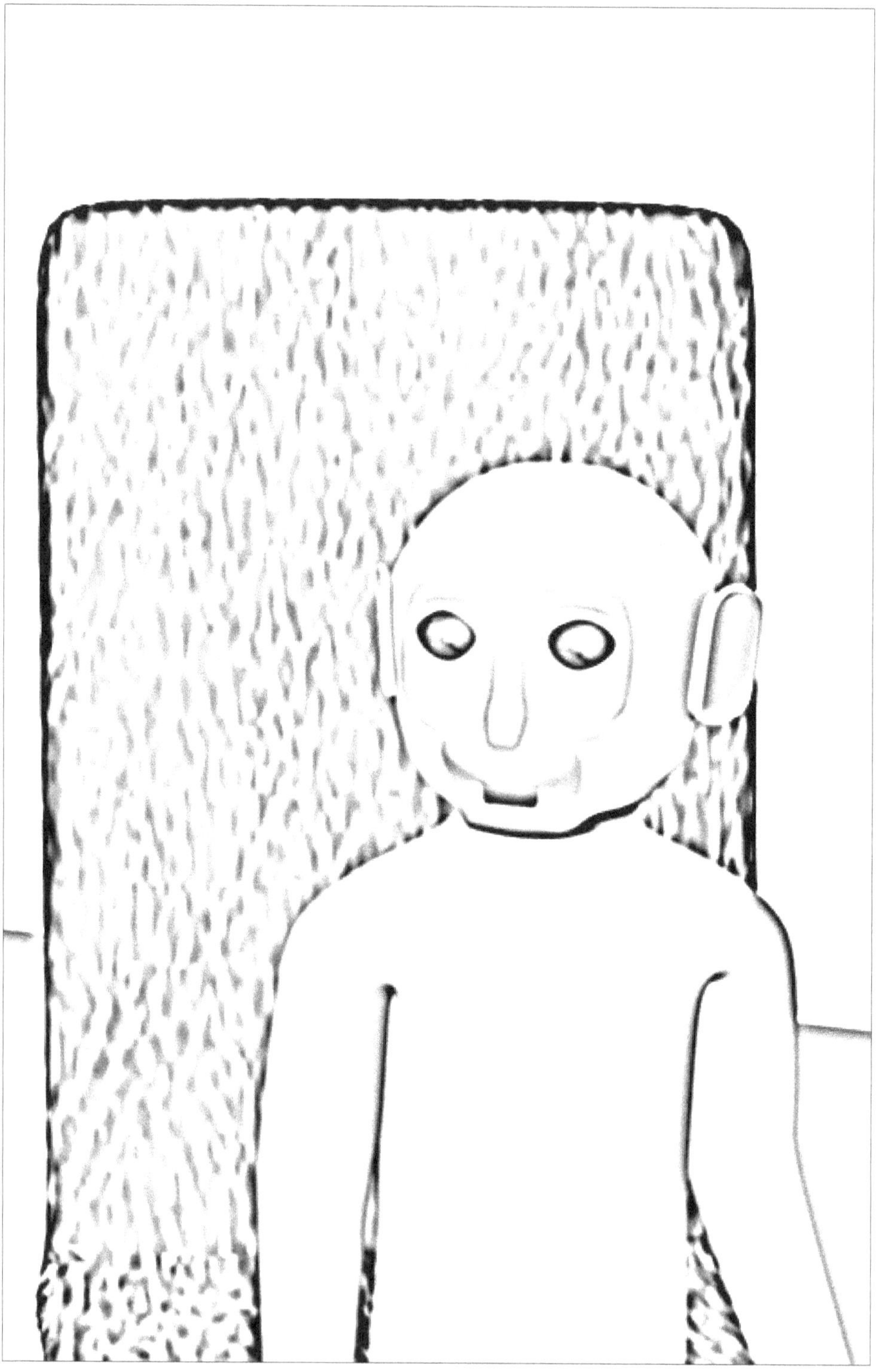

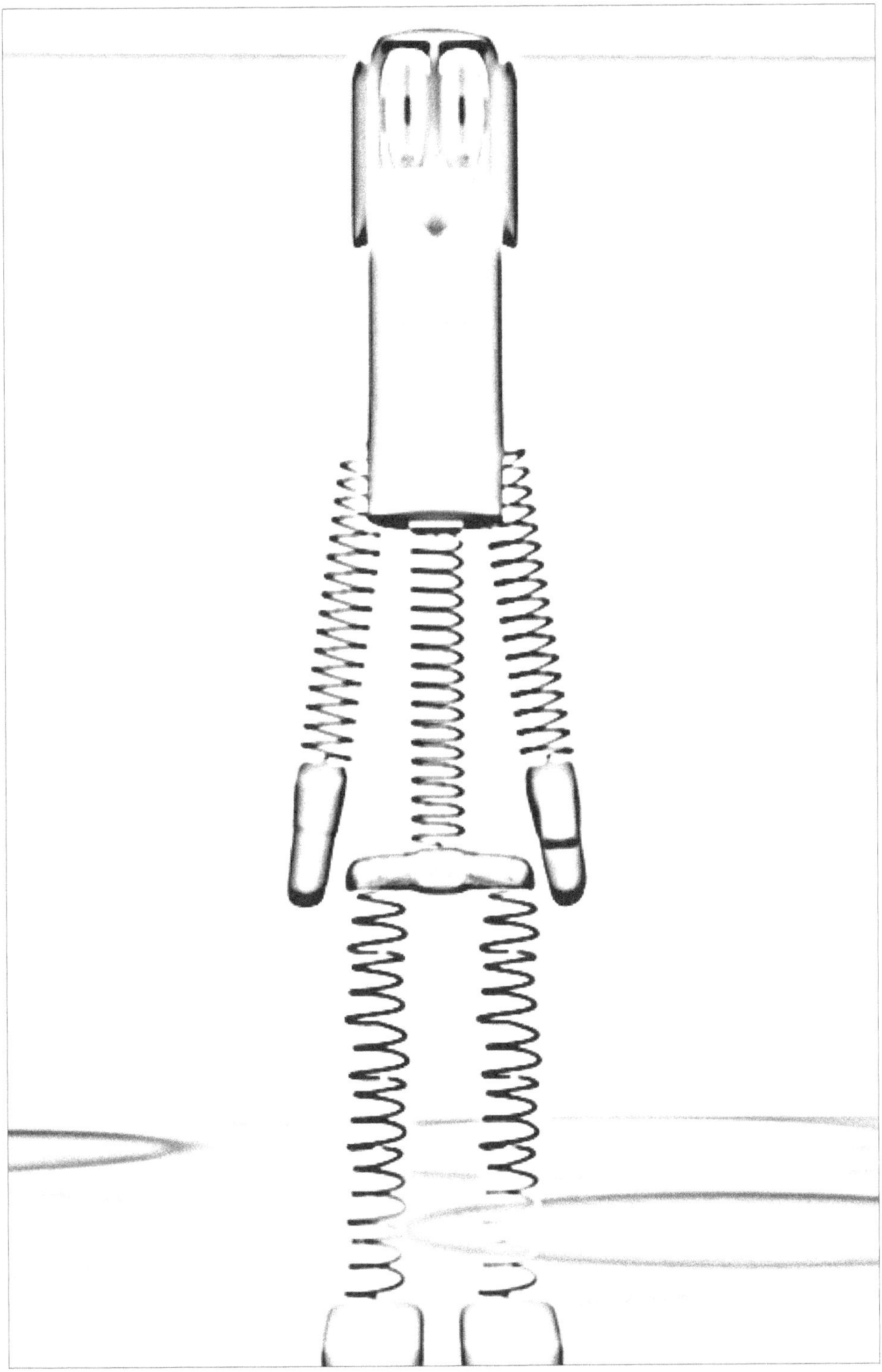

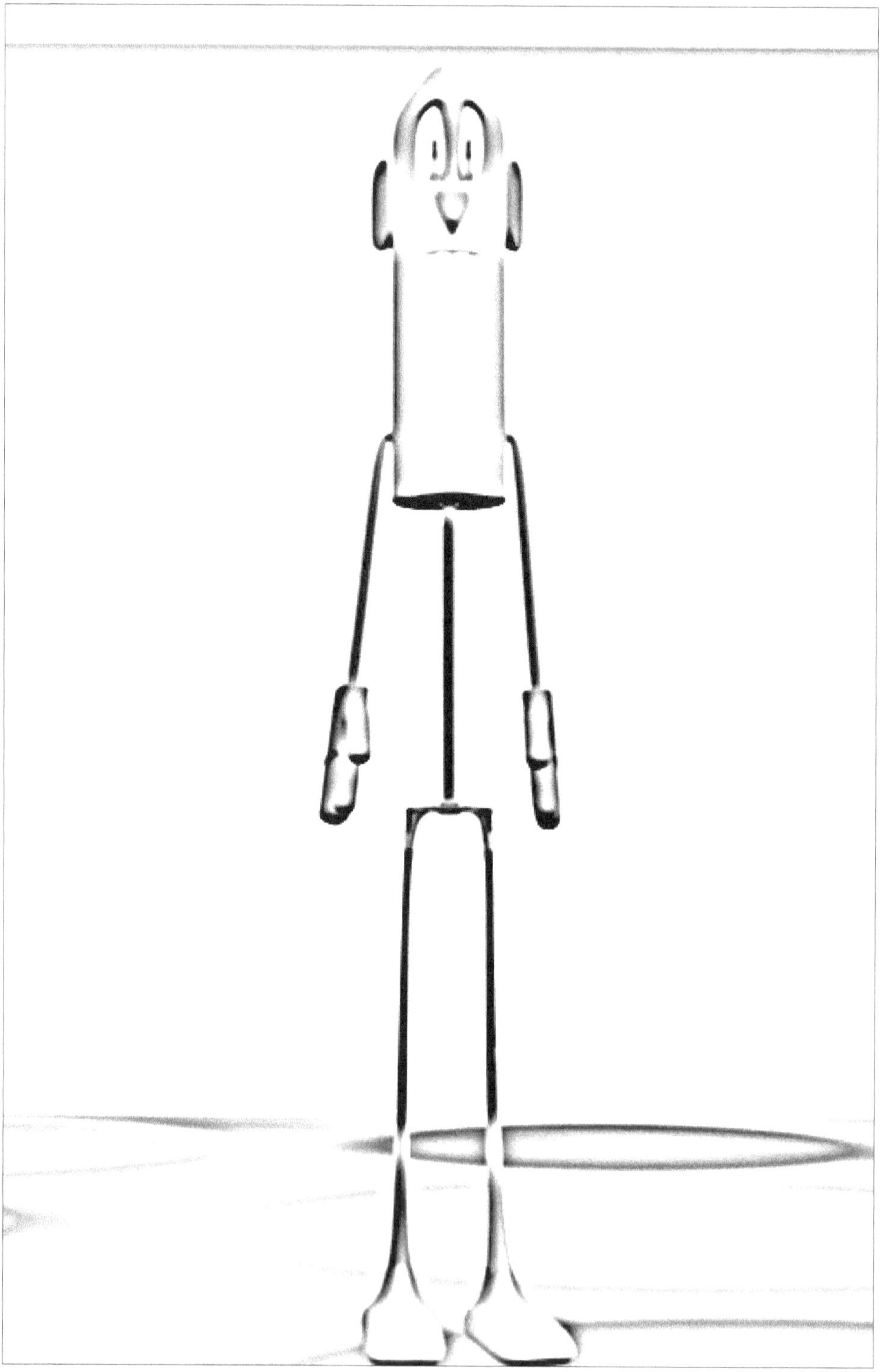

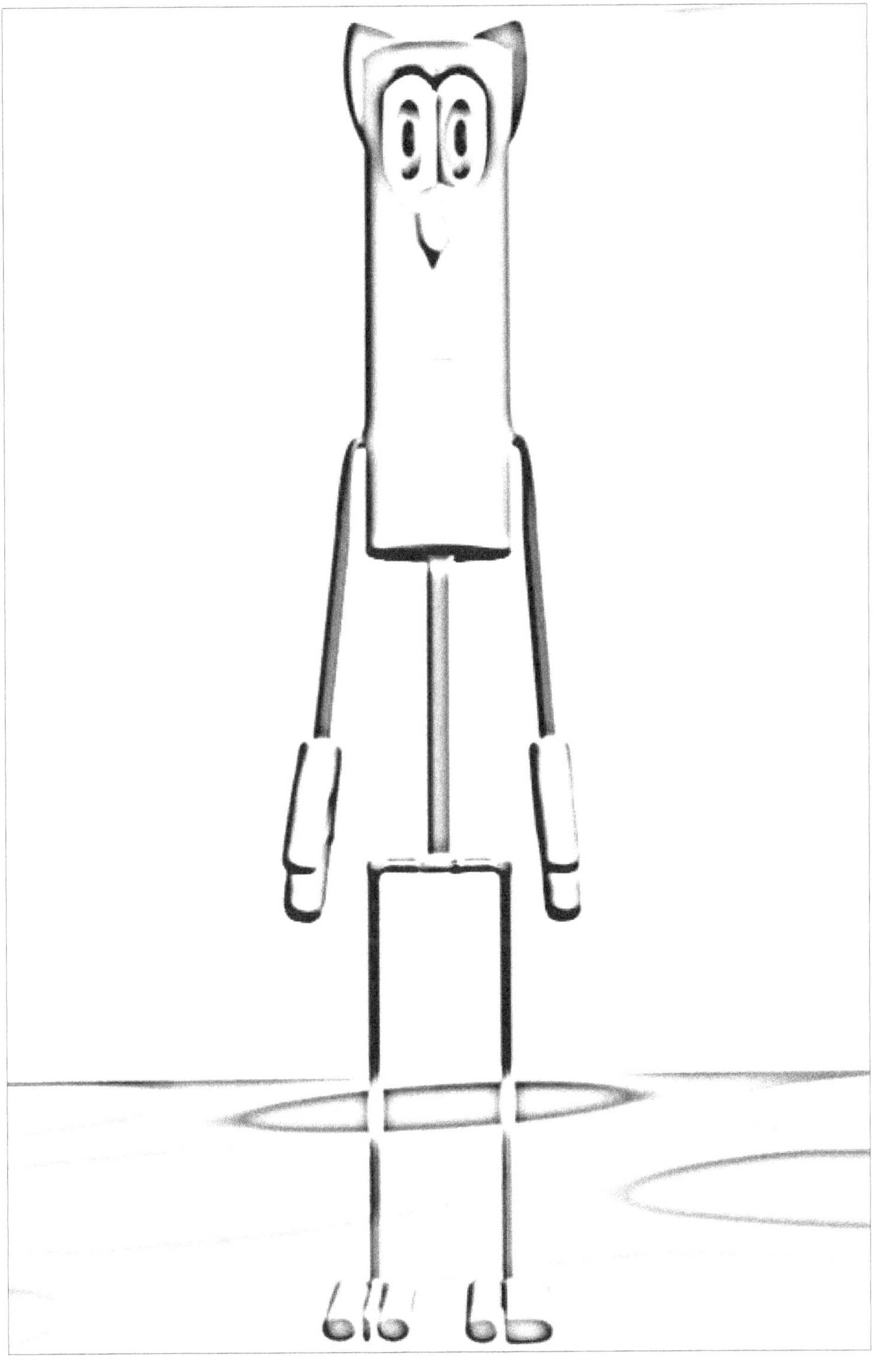

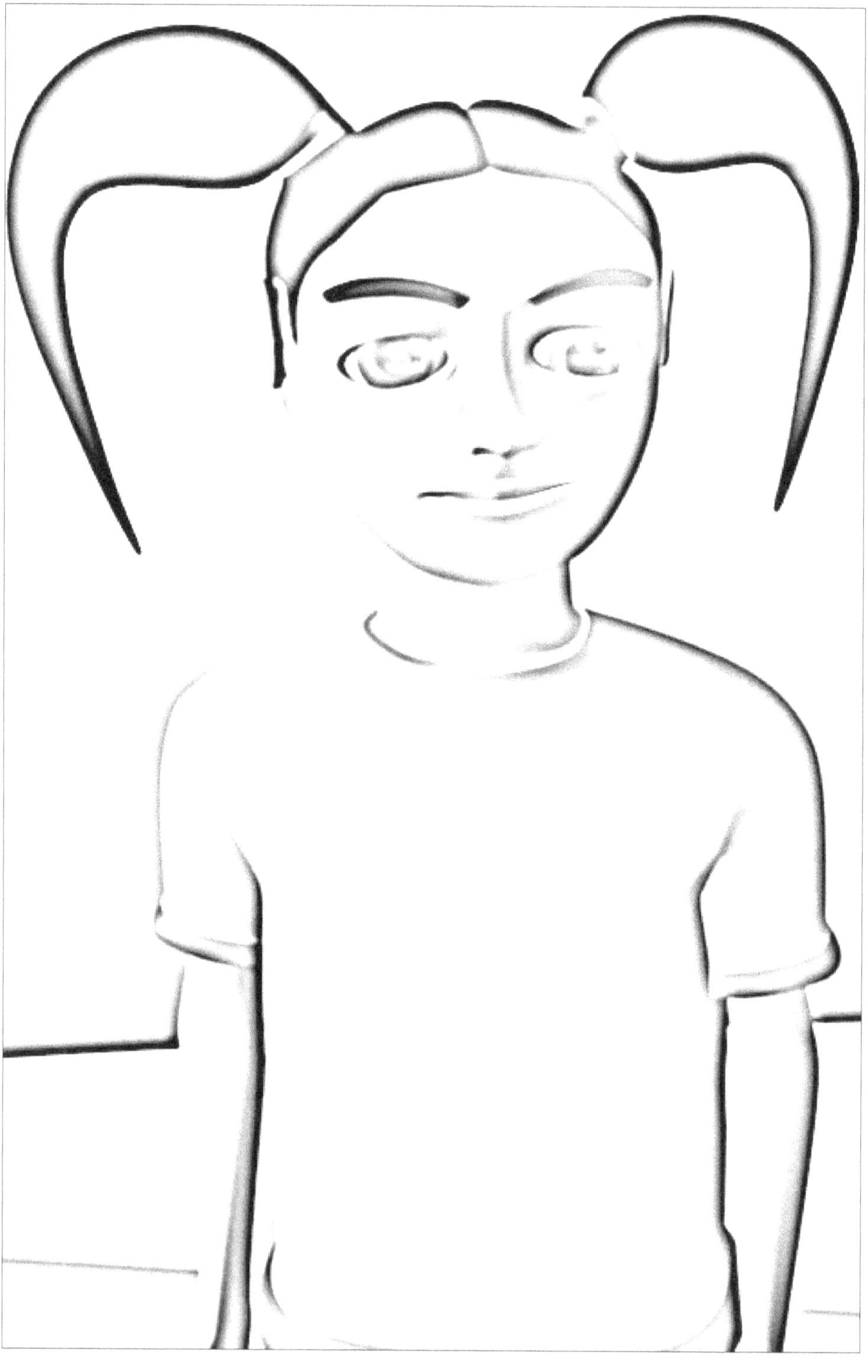

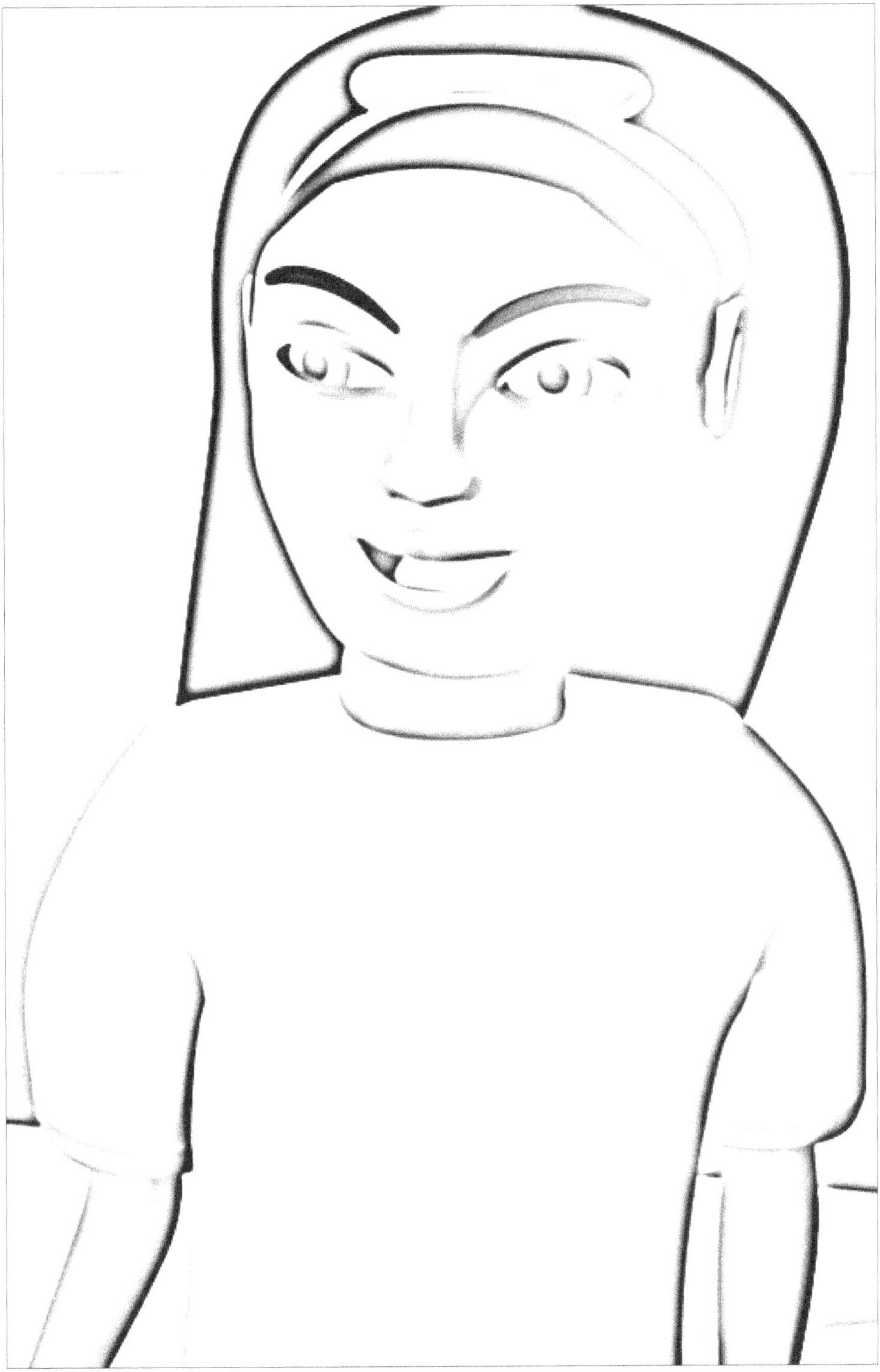

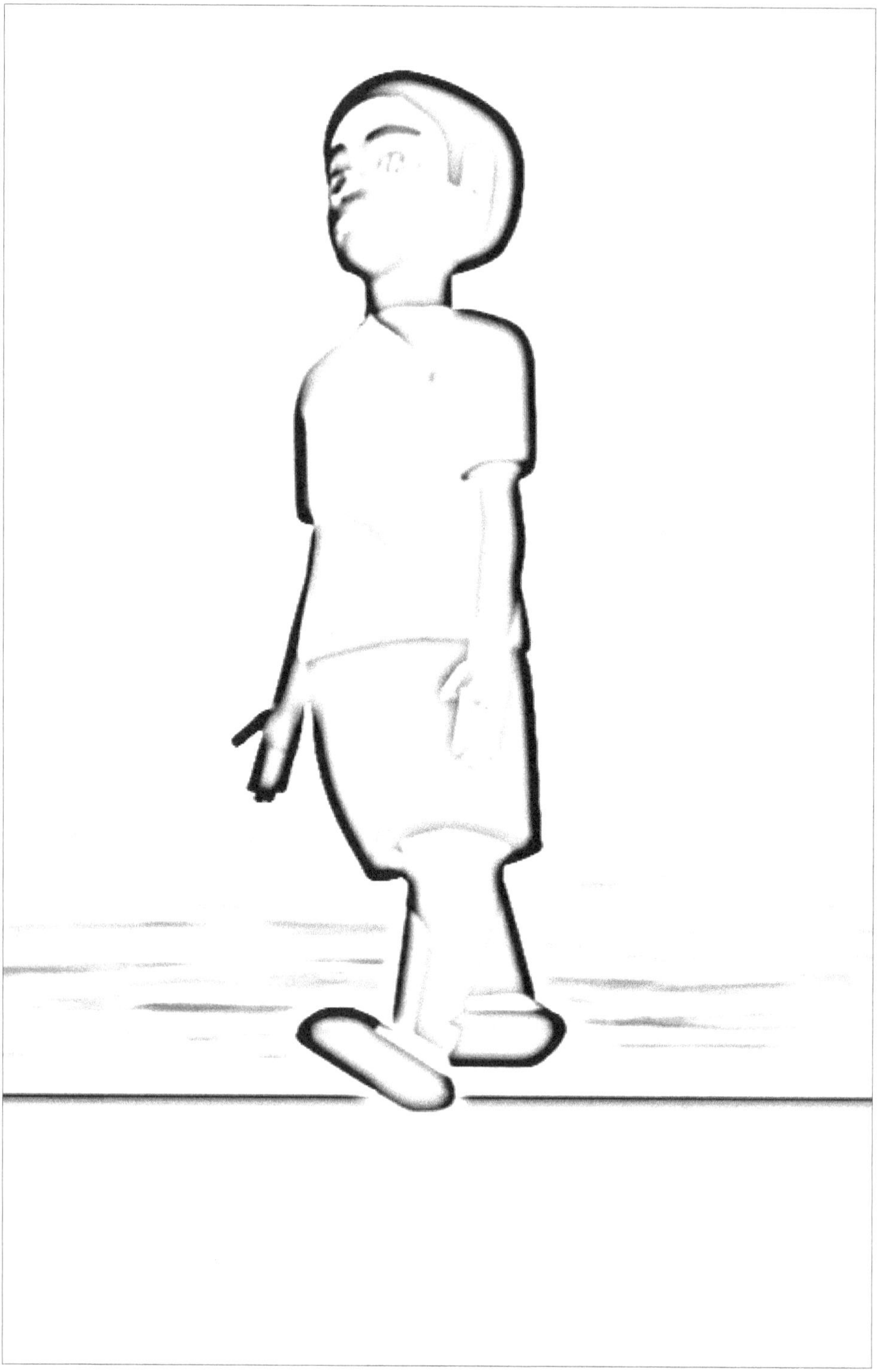

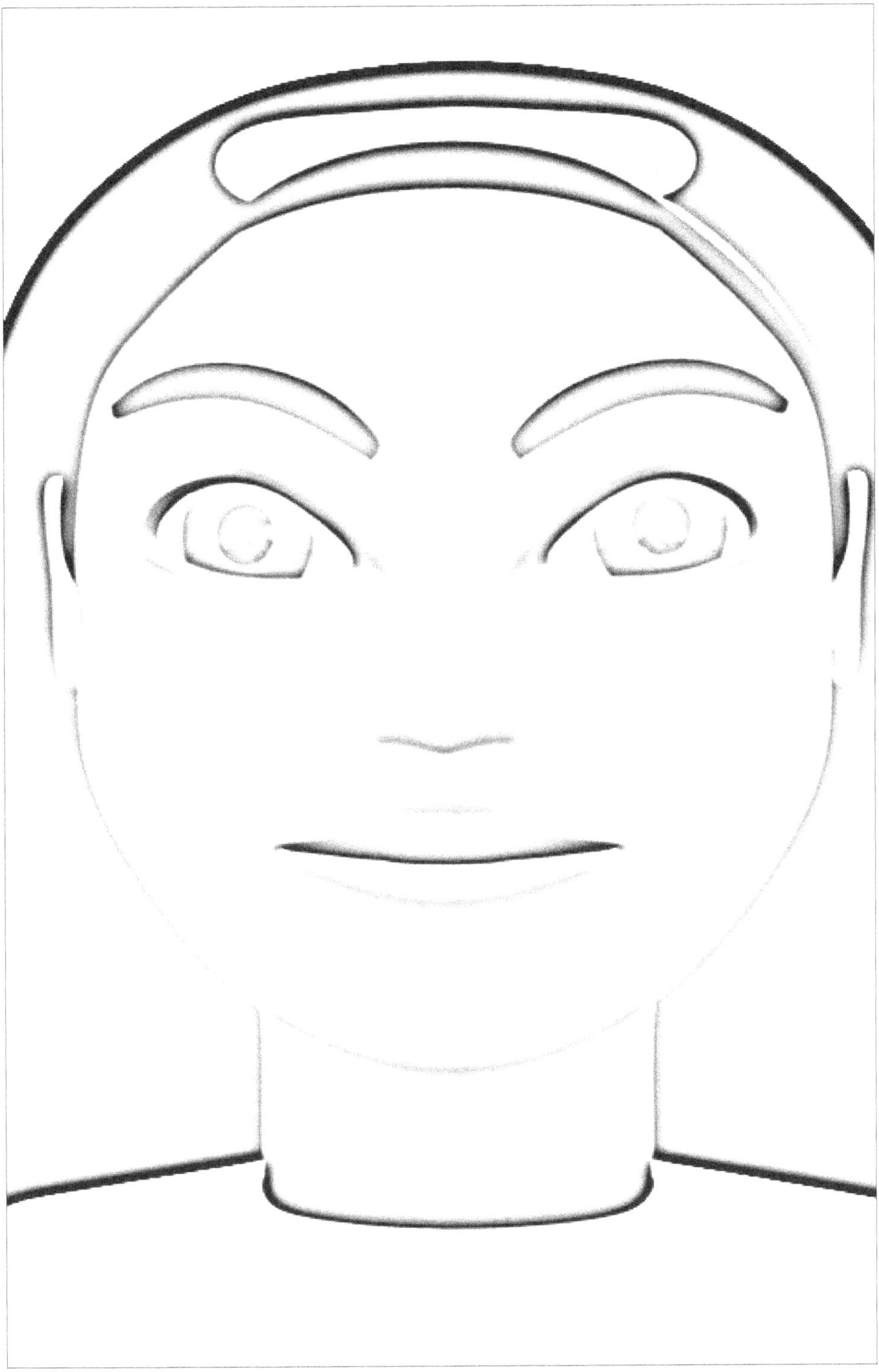

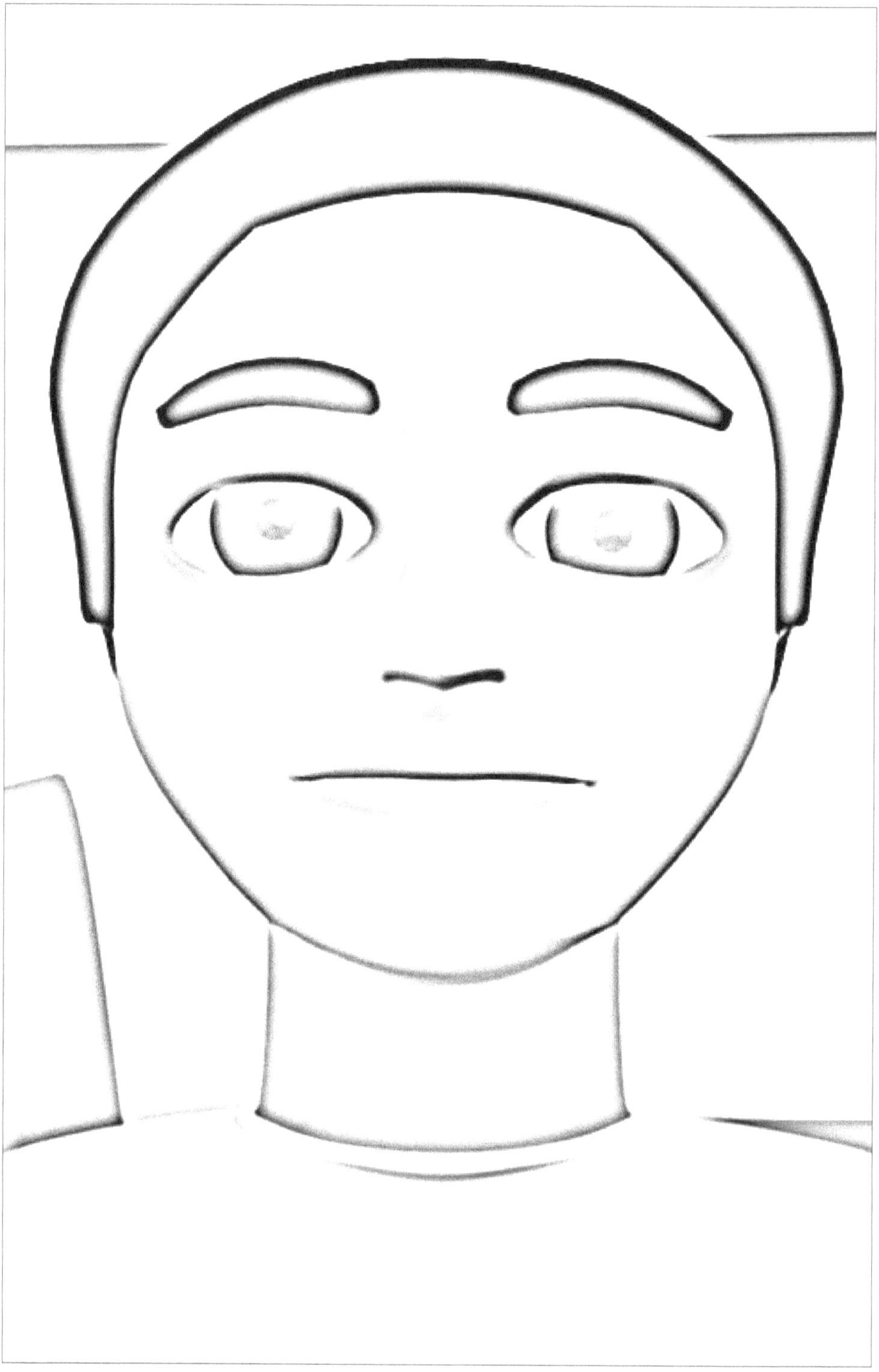

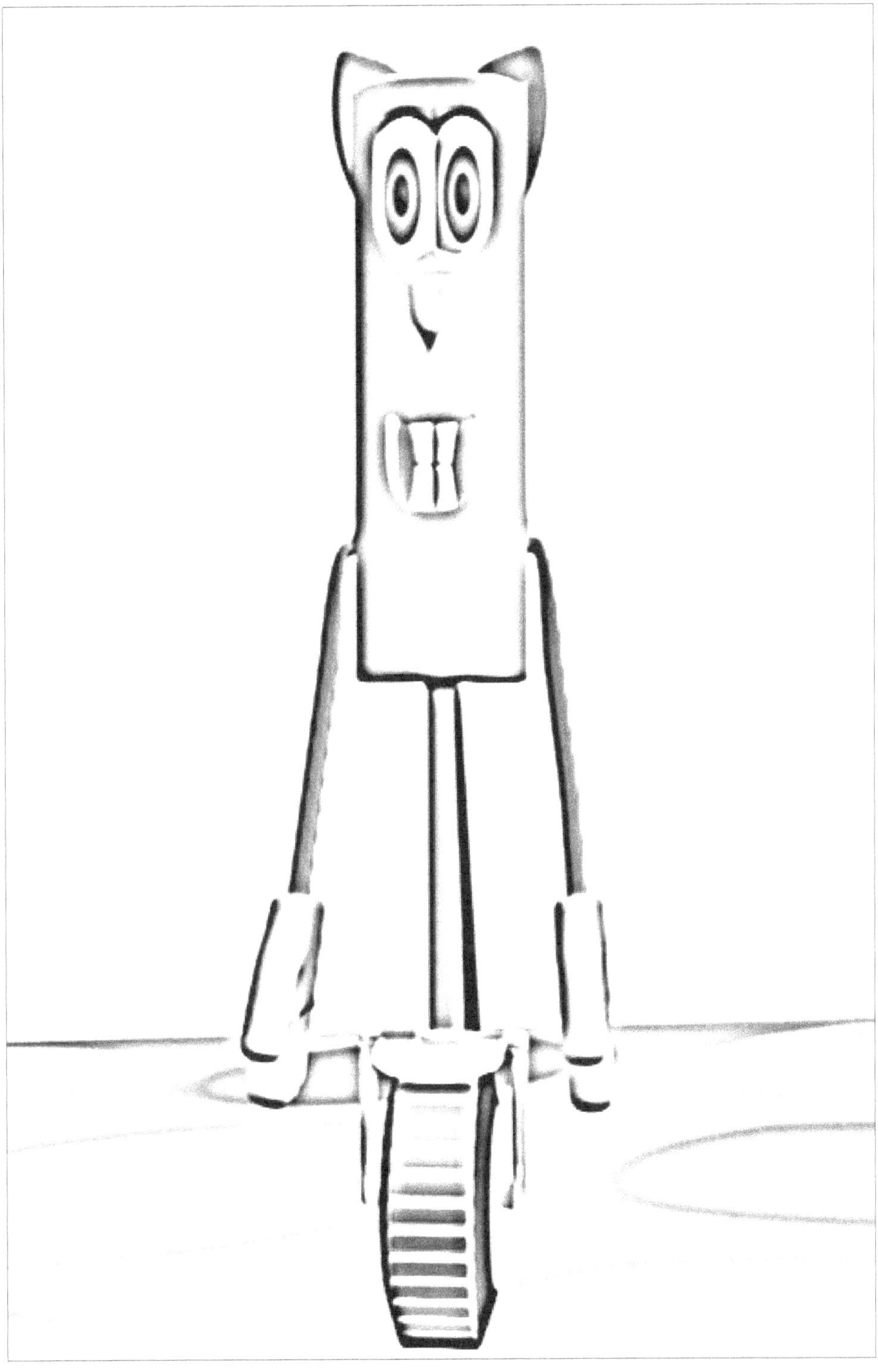

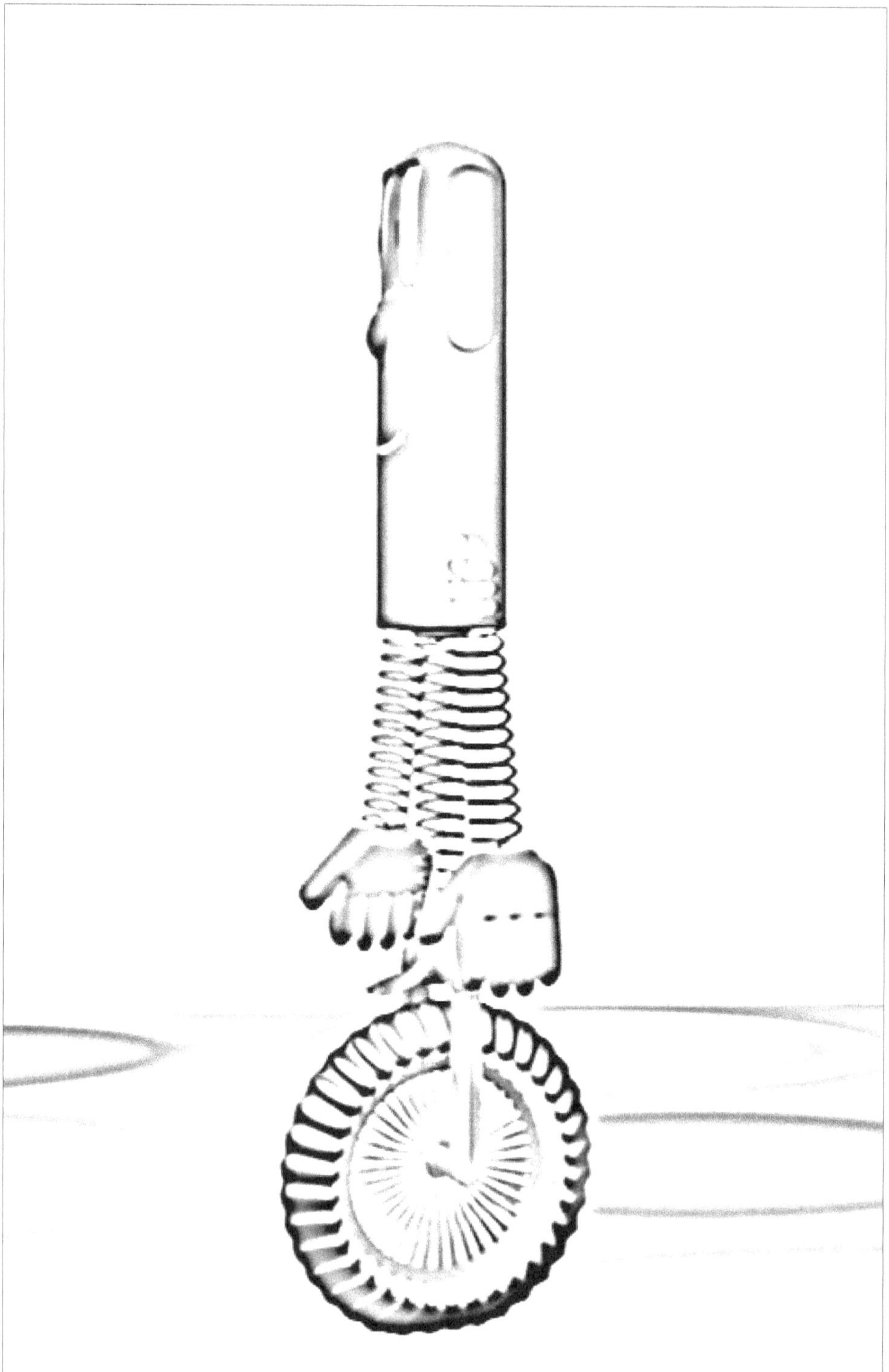

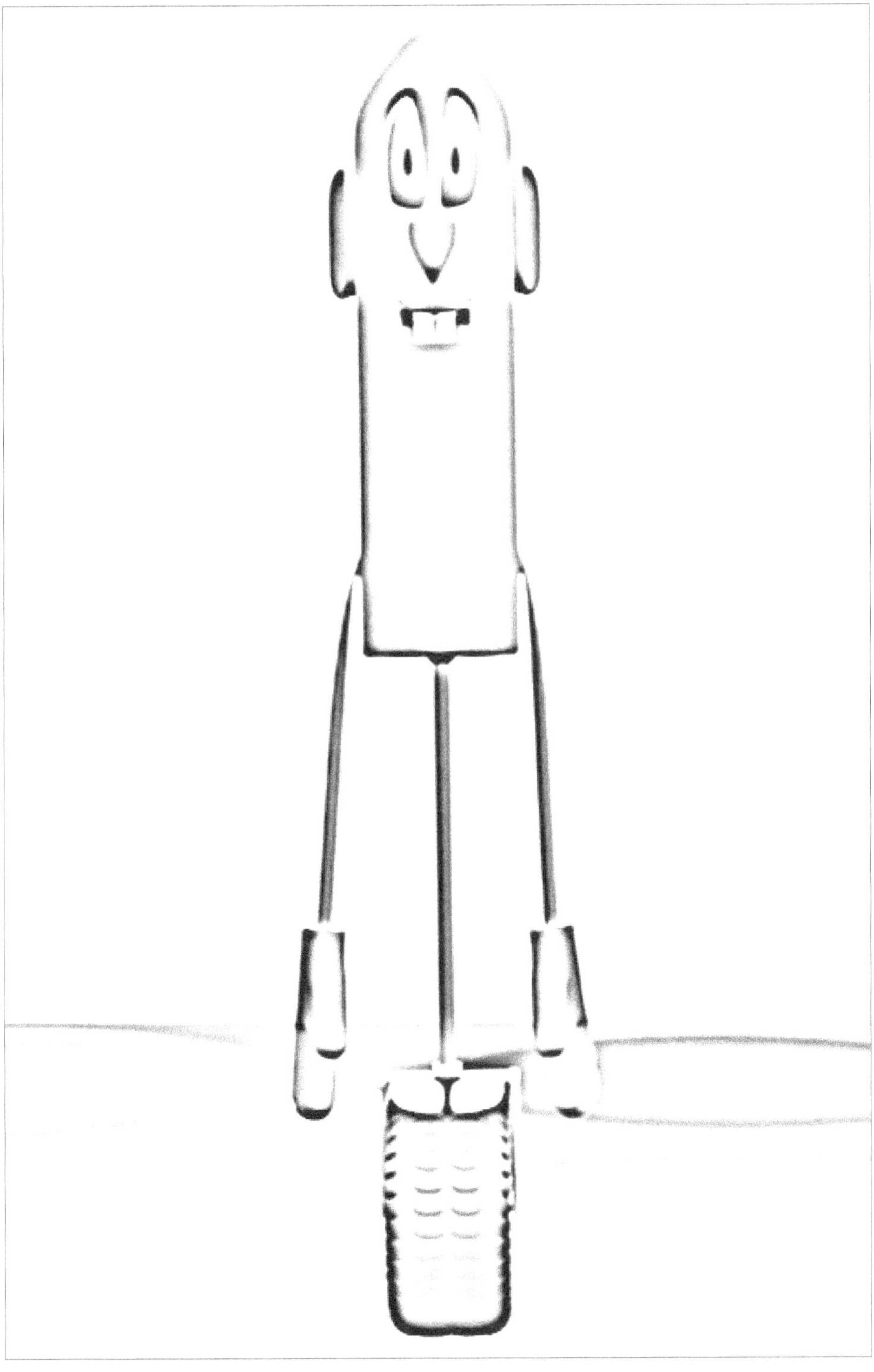

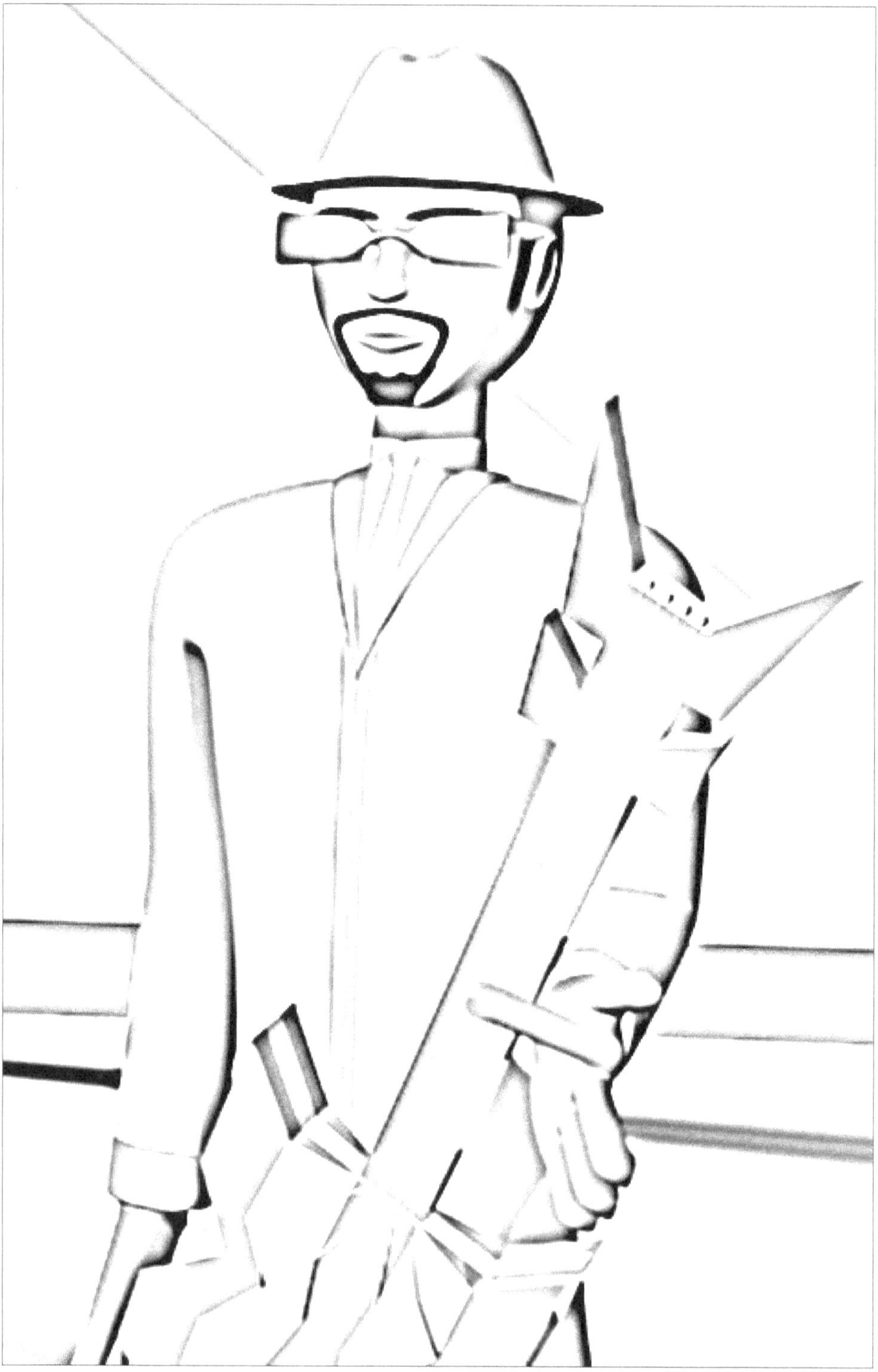

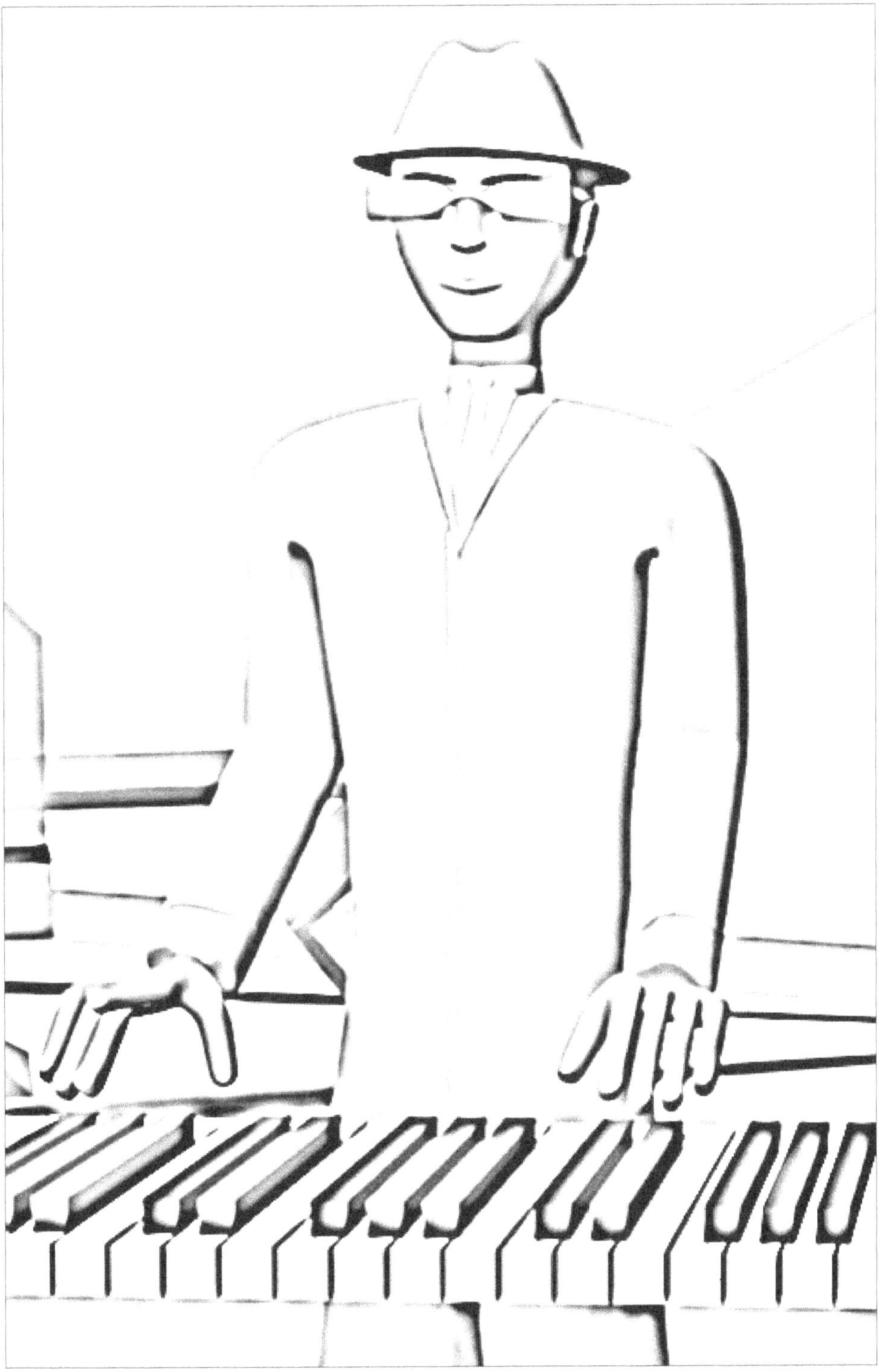

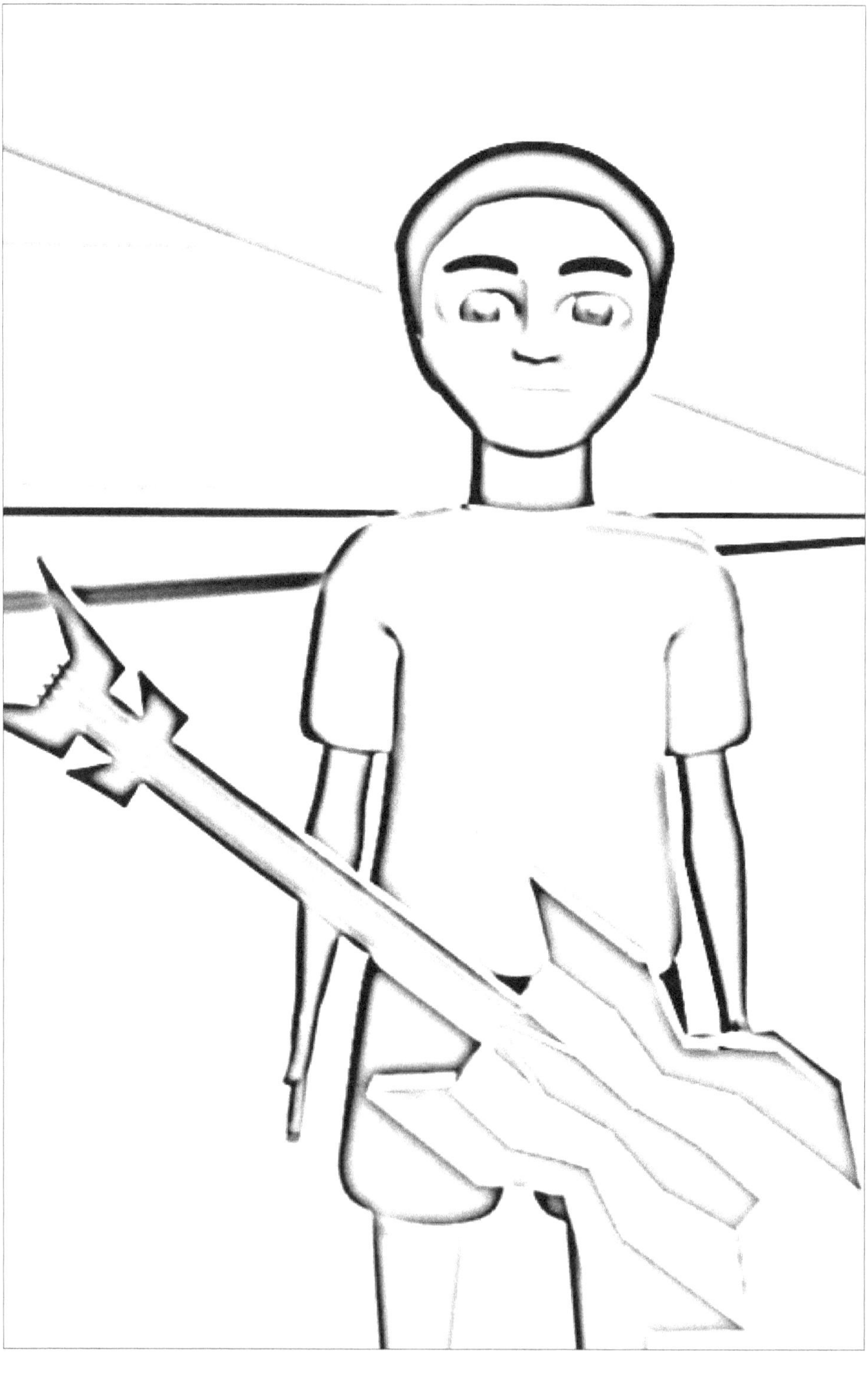

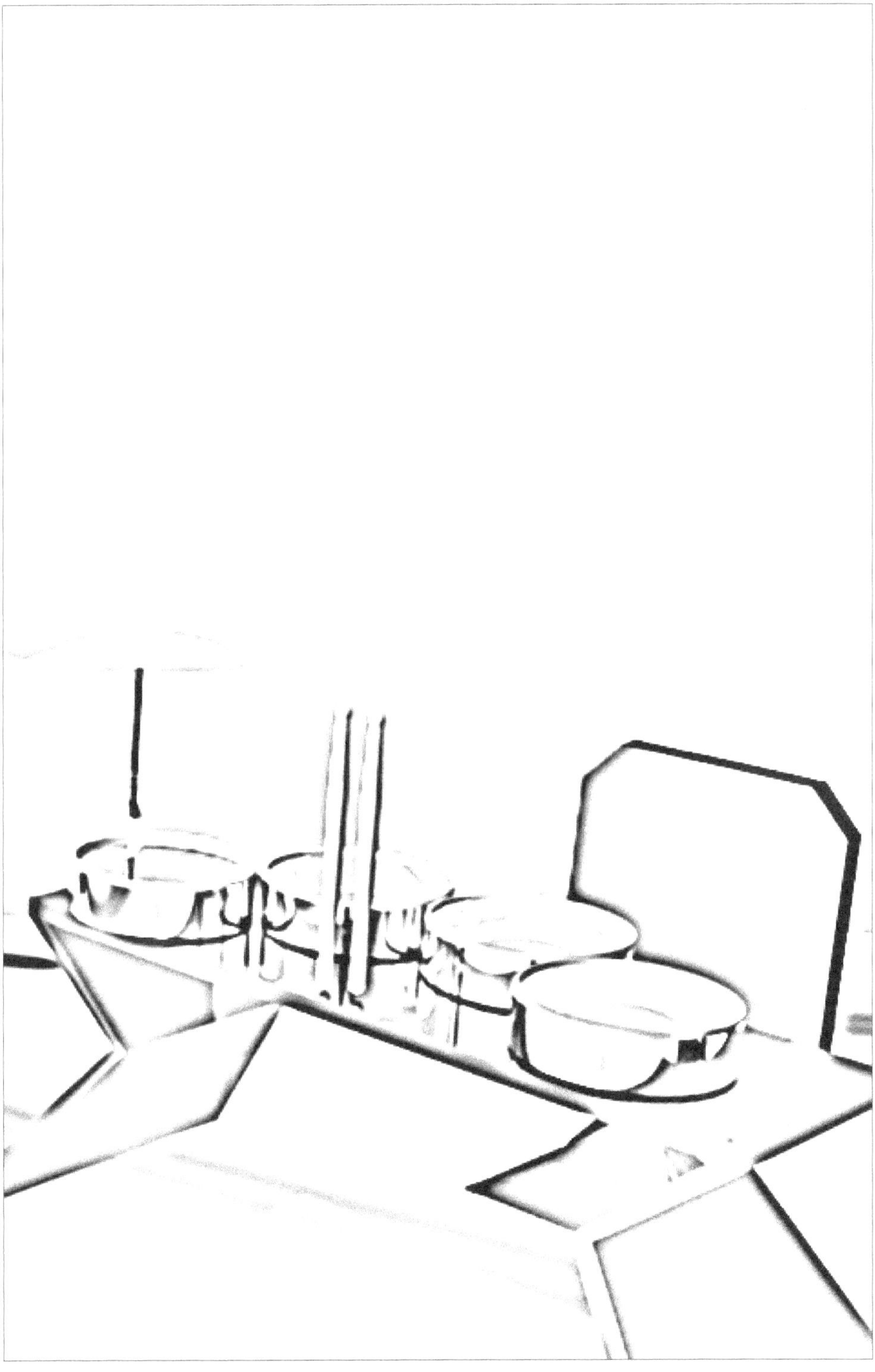

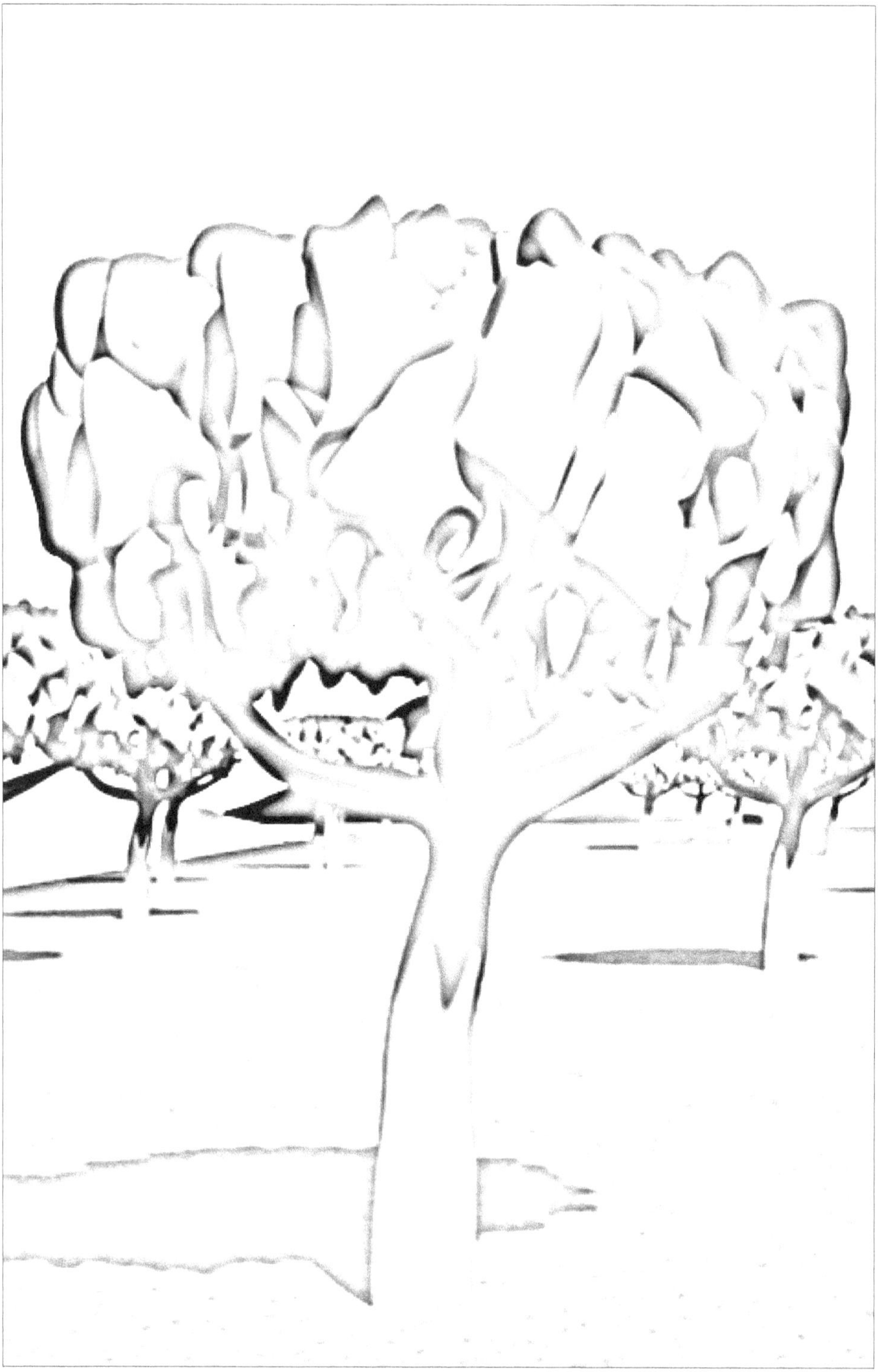

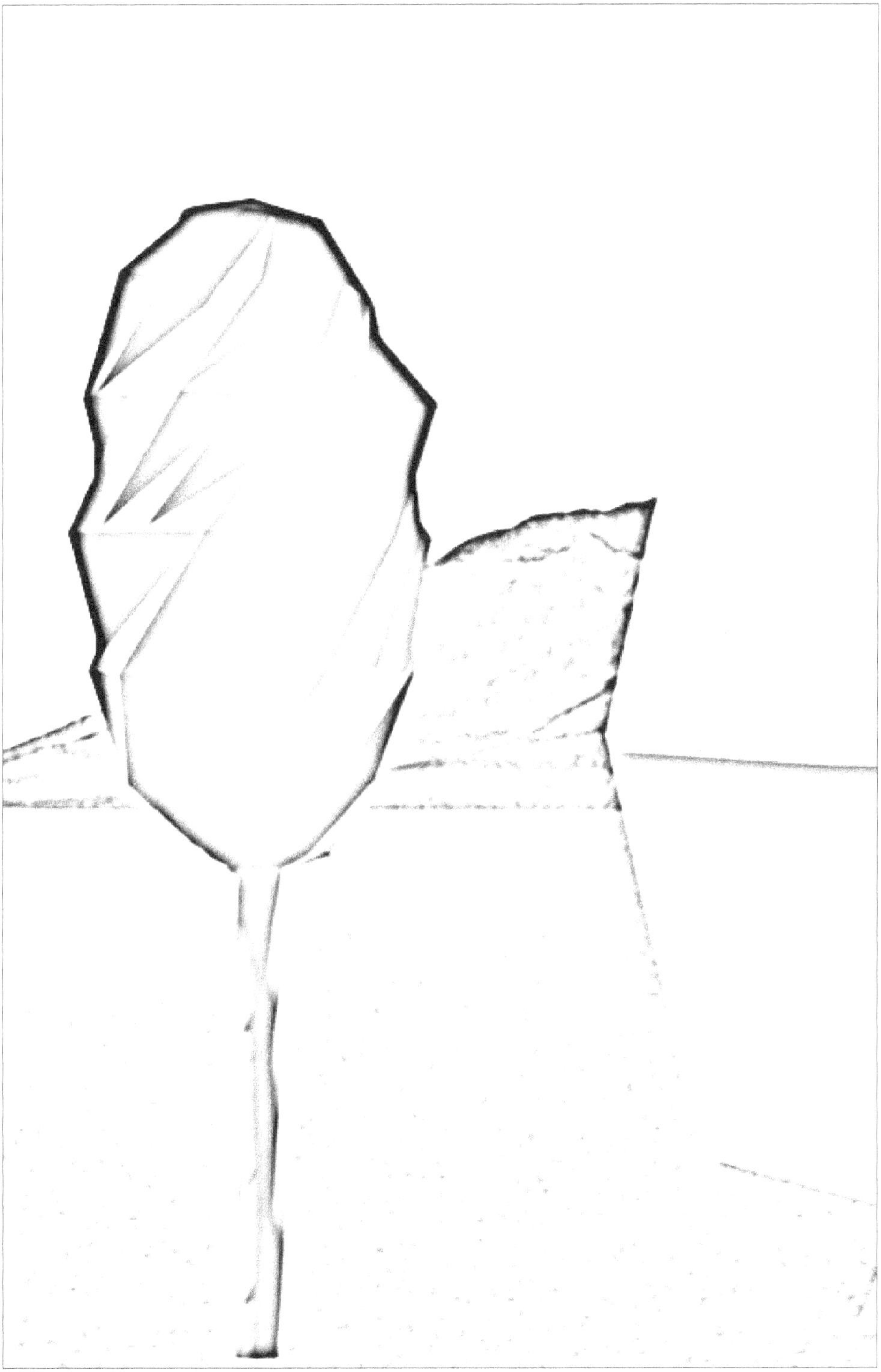

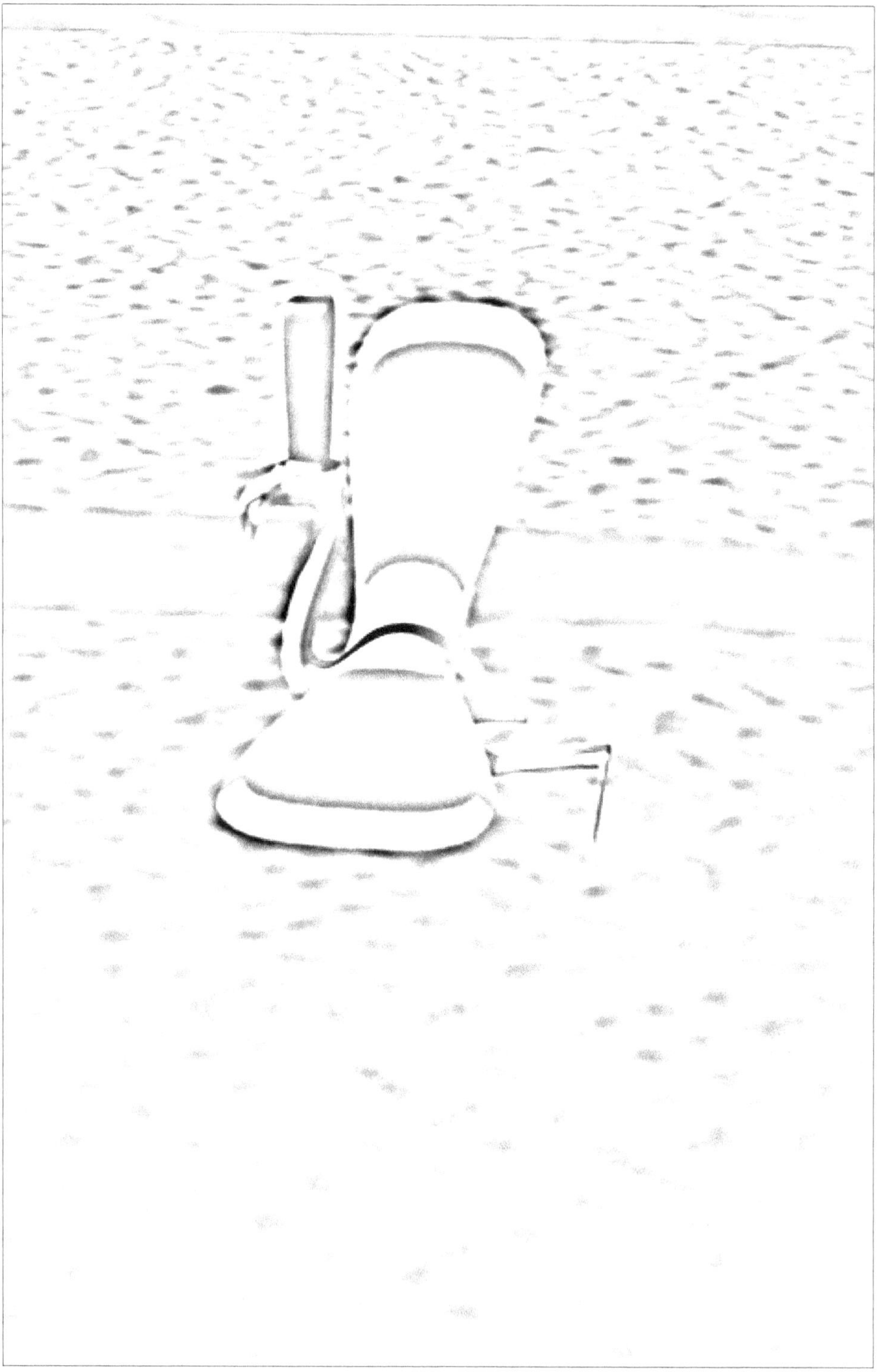

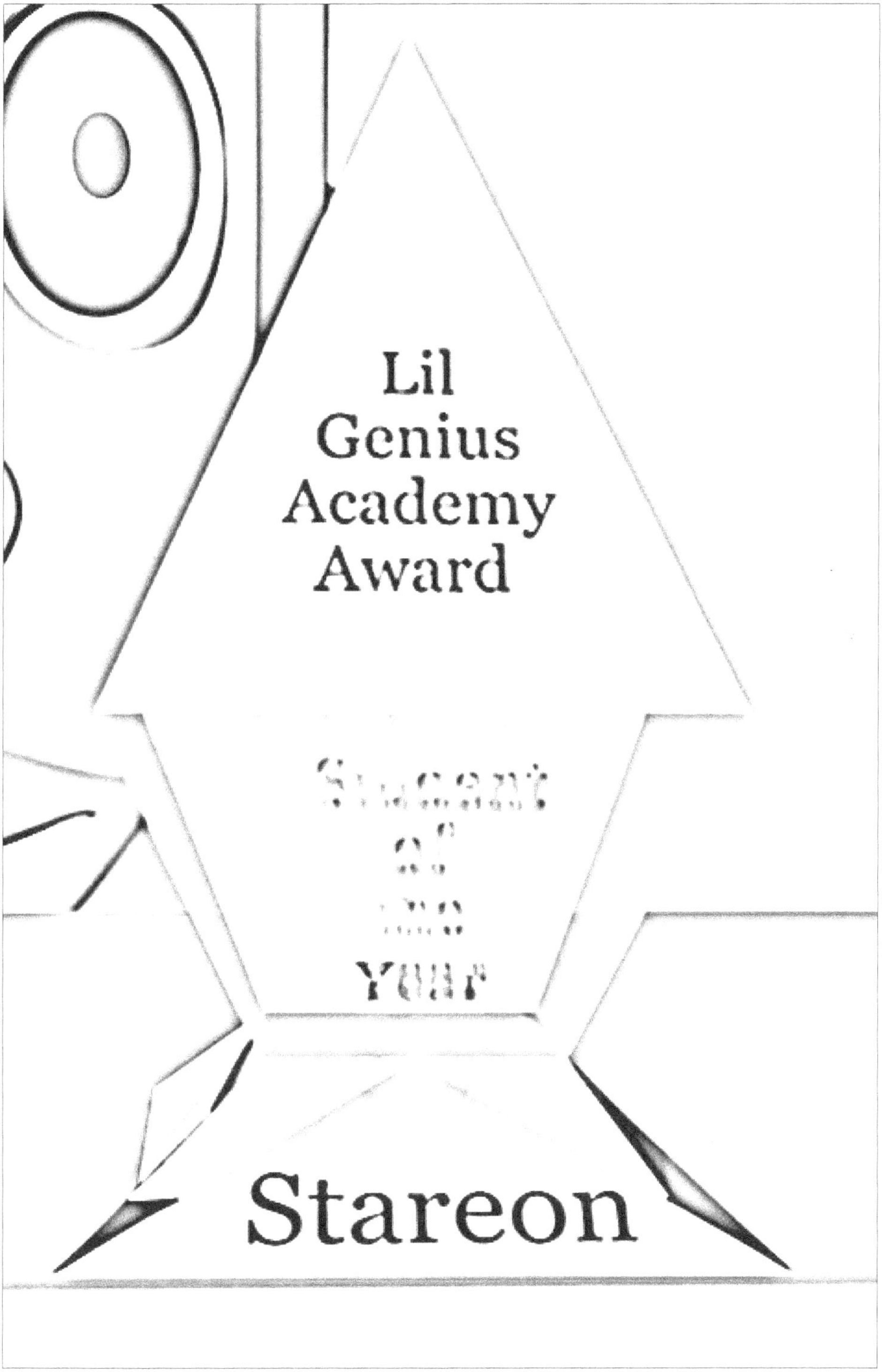
Lil
Genius
Academy
Award
Year
Stareon

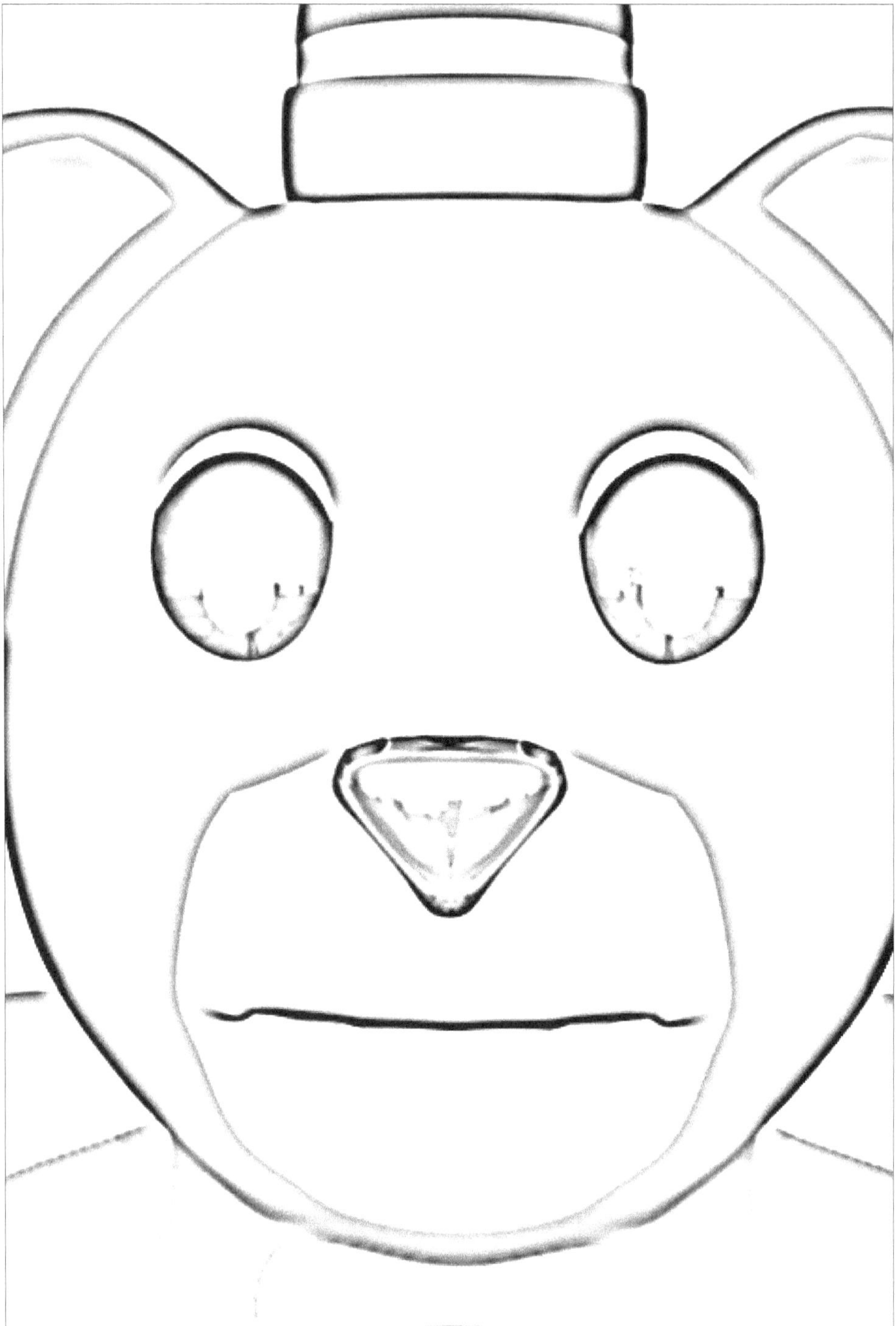

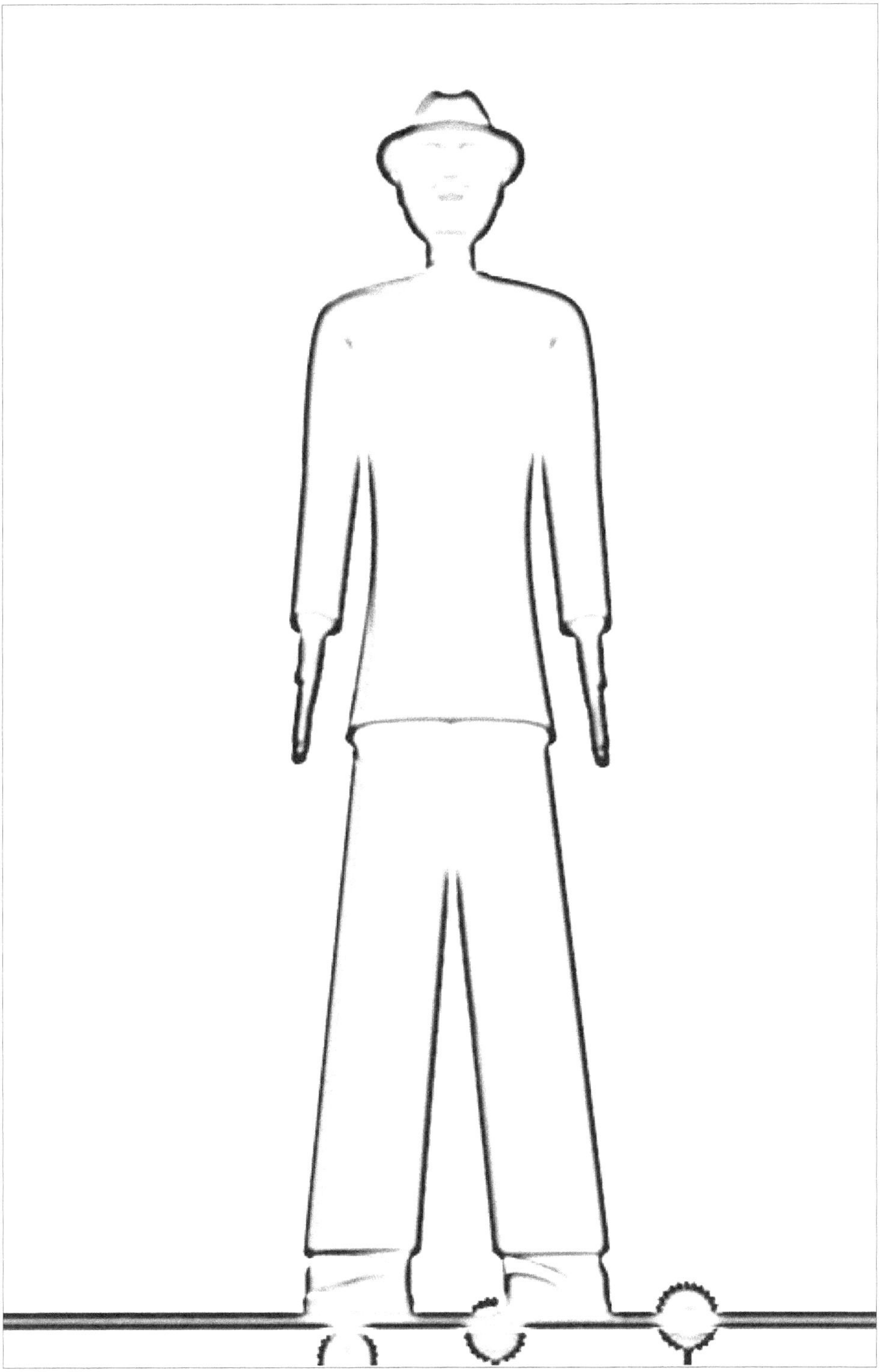

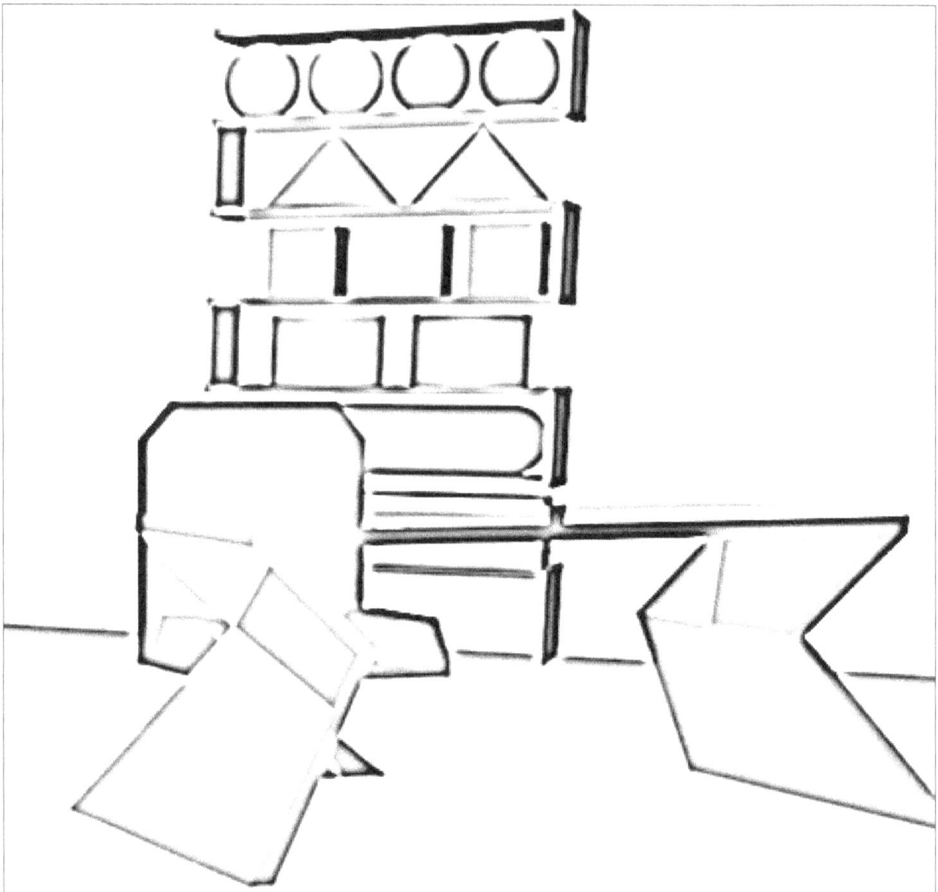

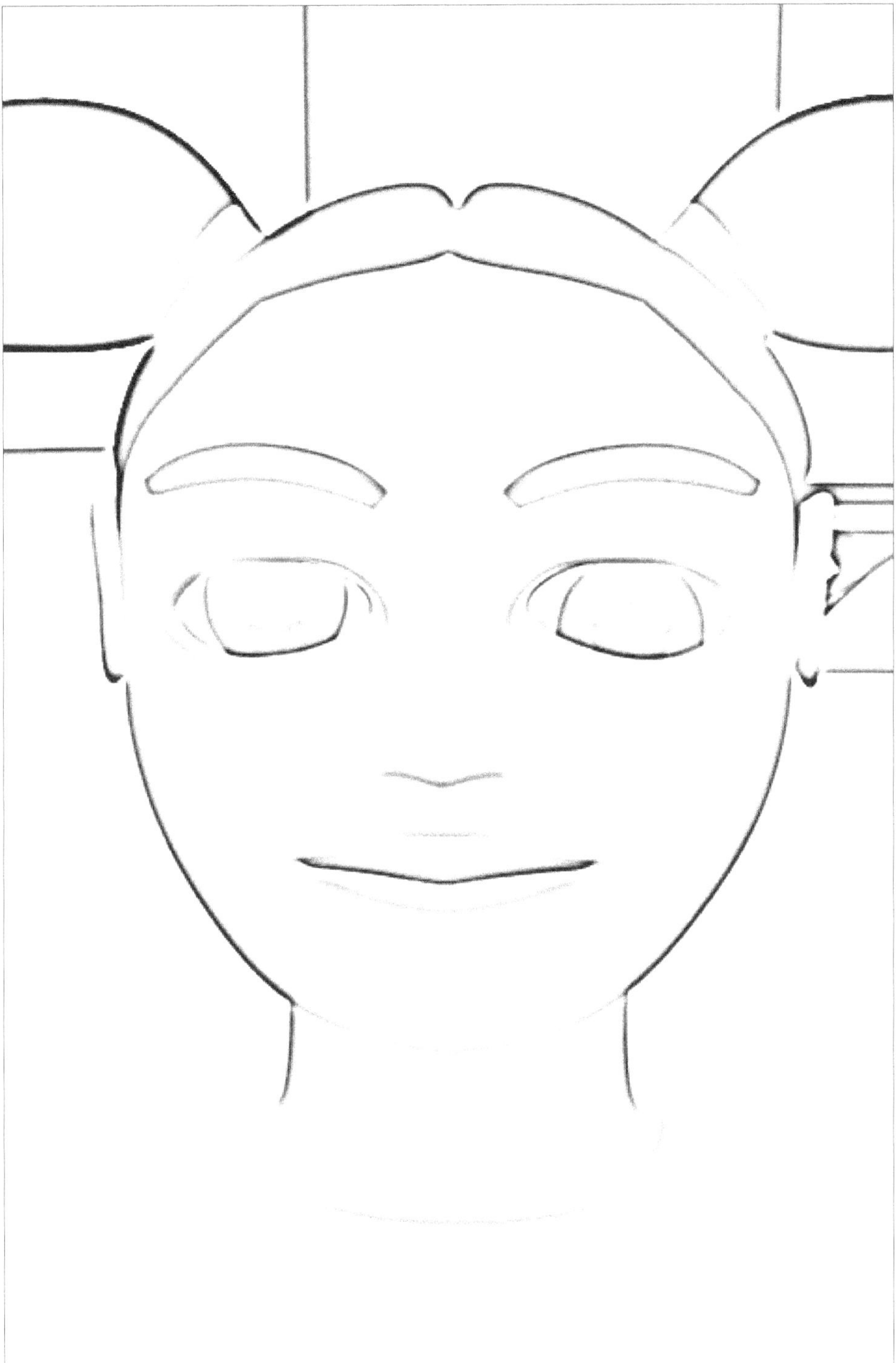

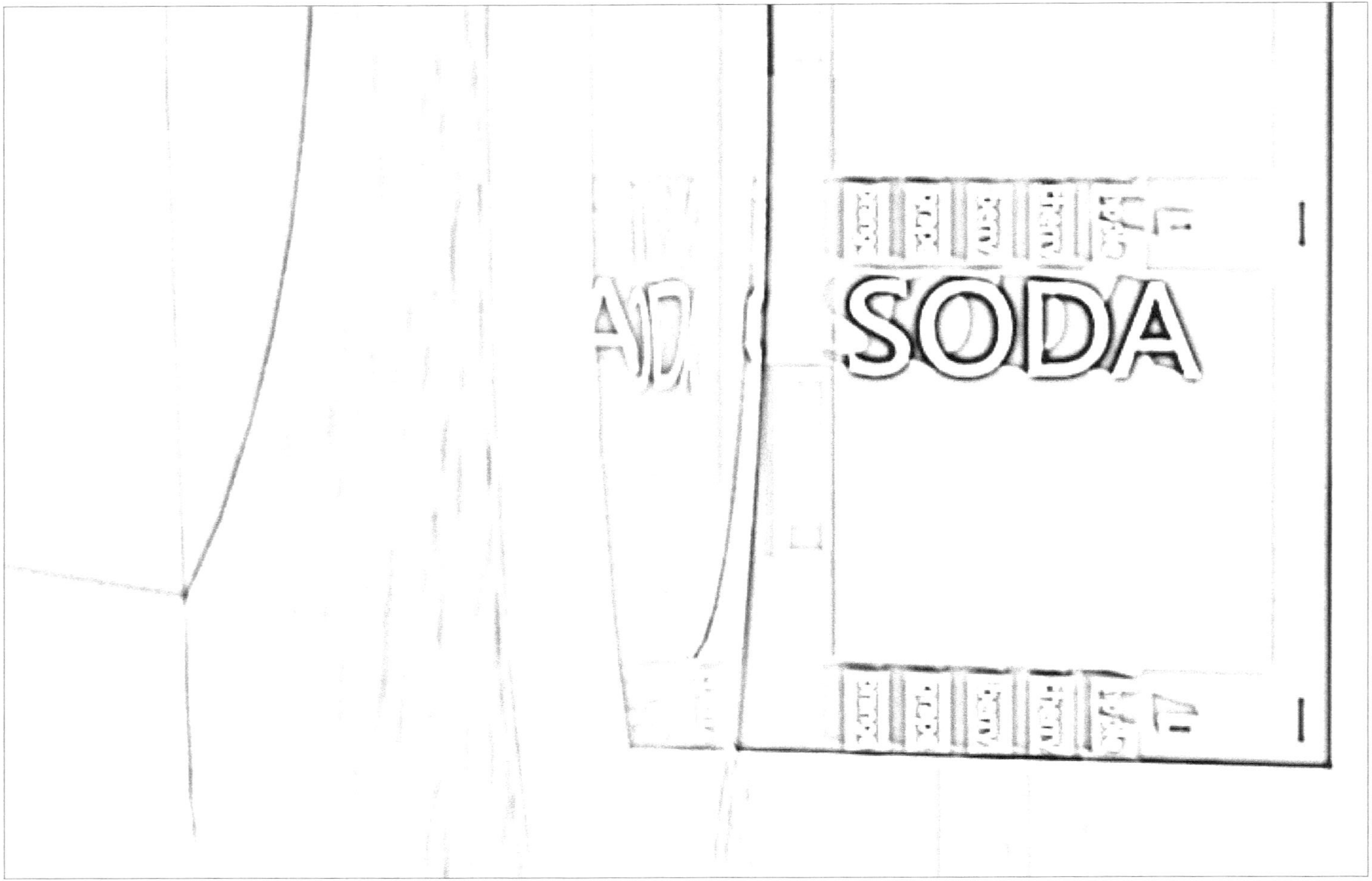
SODA

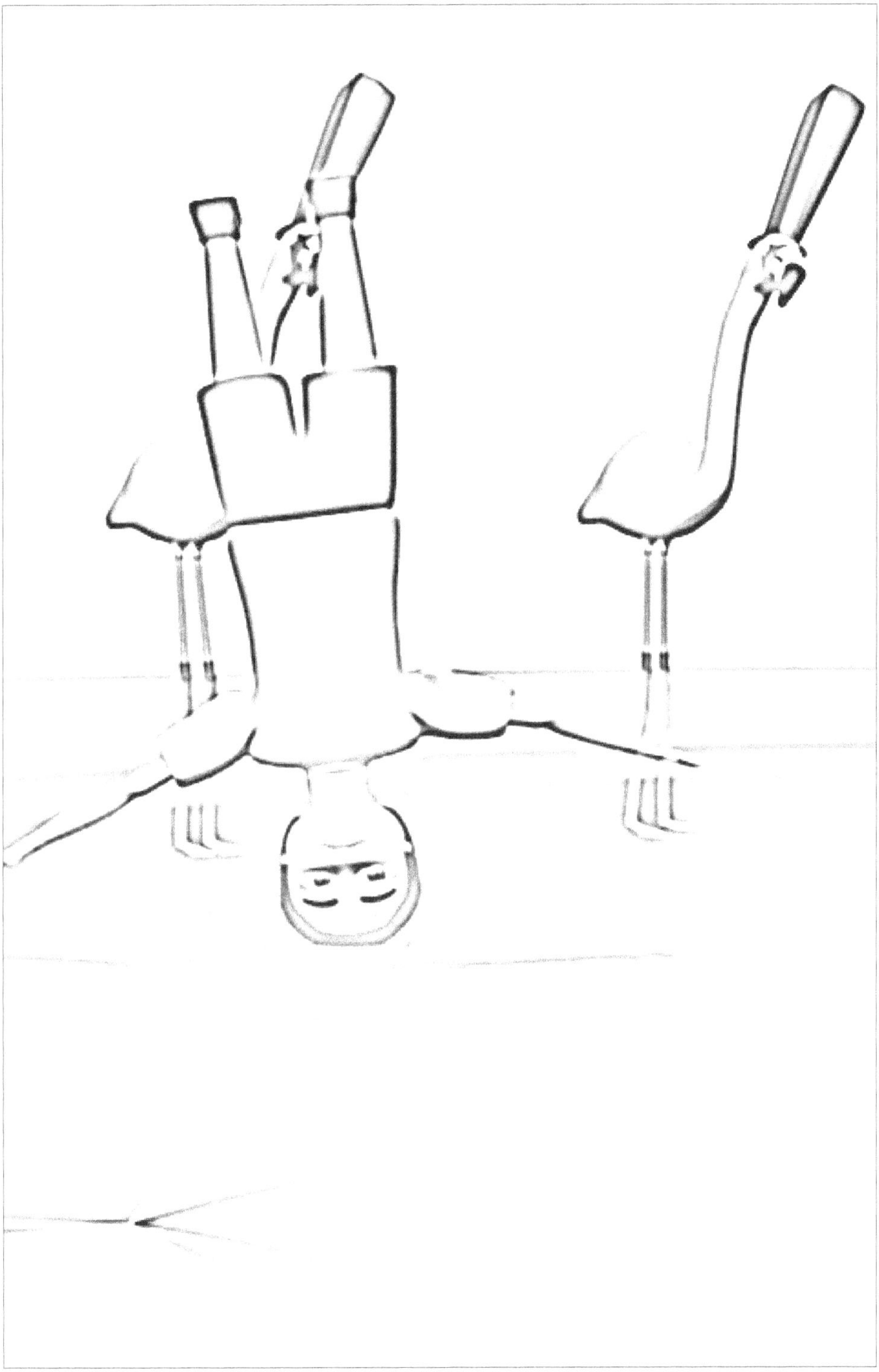

www.ingramcontent.com/pod-product-compliance
Lightning Source LLC
Chambersburg PA
CBHW030121230526
45469CB00005B/1742
9781726407601